Low pay, household resources and poverty

Jane Millar and Karen Gardiner

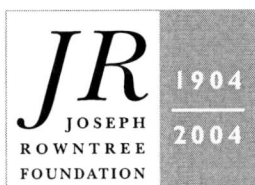

JR
JOSEPH
ROWNTREE
FOUNDATION
1904
2004

The **Joseph Rowntree Foundation** has supported this project as part of its programme of research and innovative development projects, which it hopes will be of value to policy makers, practitioners and service users. The facts presented and views expressed in this report are, however, those of the authors and not necessarily those of the Foundation.

Joseph Rowntree Foundation
The Homestead
40 Water End
York YO30 6WP
Website: www.jrf.org.uk

UNIVERSITY OF
BATH

CASP   Centre for the Analysis
of Social Policy

The Centre for the Analysis of Social Policy is the focus for social policy research across the disciplines and different subject areas of the Faculty of Humanities and Social Sciences at the University of Bath. See http://www.bath.ac.uk/casp

© University of Bath, Centre for the Analysis of Social Policy 2004

First published 2004 by the Joseph Rowntree Foundation

ISBN 1 85935 257 X   (paperback)
ISBN 1 85935 258 8   (pdf: available at www.jrf.org.uk)

A CIP catalogue record for this report is available from the British Library.

Cover design by Adkins Design

Prepared and printed by:
York Publishing Services Ltd
64 Hallfield Road
Layerthorpe
York YO31 7ZQ
Tel: 01904 430033; Fax: 01904 430868; Website: www.yps-publishing.co.uk

Further copies of this report, or any other JRF publication, can be obtained either from the JRF website (www.jrf.org.uk/bookshop/) or from our distributor, York Publishing Services Ltd, at the above address.

Contents

List of tables, figures and boxes

Tables

Figures

Boxes

Acknowledgements

The authors thank the Joseph Rowntree Foundation for funding this research. The Advisory Group, chaired by Chris Goulden of the JRF, and including Fran Bennett, Rebecca Endean, Donald Hirsch, Abigail McKnight and Holly Sutherland, shared their knowledge and gave us excellent advice, for which we are very grateful. Thanks to Faith Howard at the University of Bath for her help in preparing the report. Thanks also to the Department for Work and Pensions for providing the population totals to generate grossing-up weights, and to the Office for National Statistics (2002) for collecting and the ESRC Data Archive for providing the Family Expenditure Survey data. The data providers and collectors bear no responsibility for our analysis or interpretation of the data. Crown copyright material is reproduced with the kind permission of the Controller of the HMSO and the Queen's Printer for Scotland.

1 Introduction: individual low pay and household poverty

There are about 27 million people in employment in Britain, about three-quarters of the working-age population, and for most their jobs are a source of an adequate income, of status and of security. Some working people are extremely well paid. Most earn enough to maintain a good lifestyle. Relatively few people in full-time jobs are poor. Since 1997, the government has been strongly promoting the view that 'work is the best form of welfare' and vigorously pursuing a policy agenda to promote paid work, to make work possible and to make work pay. In their recent analysis of the government's micro-economic policy objectives, Balls *et al.* (2004) reinforce the point. Paid work, they argue, is the 'single most effective means of avoiding poverty, both now and in the future' (Balls *et al.*, 2004, p. 188), and so providing 'employment opportunity for all' is central to the government objective of creating a fairer and more socially inclusive society.

But the labour market is very diverse and employment opportunities very unequal. There are many people in jobs that are low-paid, part-time, insecure and with limited scope for advancement. Most people who move into work after being unemployed or otherwise inactive do so at wage levels well below the average. Some are locked into a 'low pay/no pay' cycle, and wage progression may be slow or non-existent, especially for people without skills or qualifications (McKnight, 2002; Dickens and Manning, 2003). The wage distribution has become more unequal. In 2000, the average hourly wages for men in the top tenth were £18.09 compared with £4.35 in the bottom tenth, a ratio of 4.16 to 1 compared with a ratio of 3.97 to 1 in 1990 and 2.80 to 1 in 1975 (Machin, 2003). Since the mid-1970s, real wages have hardly risen at the bottom but have risen substantially at the top (McKnight, 2002). There are large differences in wages according to educational status between men and women and between part-time and full-time workers. Accounts of working in the low-paid sector highlight the struggle to make ends meet for those in low-paid and insecure jobs (Abrams, 2002; Toynbee, 2003). For some people who are in work, or who enter work, wages alone are unlikely to be able to provide an adequate income to ensure that they can avoid poverty.

The aim of this study is to examine the extent to which paid work is indeed an 'effective means of avoiding poverty' for low-paid workers and, if so, how this is achieved. Hence, we are interested in both individual and household circumstances: whereas low wages are an individual characteristic, poverty as usually measured depends upon all sources of household income brought in by all household members. We start by looking at pay, specifically at hourly wages and at the extent and risk of low hourly pay according to gender, age and family type. Wages are the basic component of income for working people, and so the level of pay is the starting point for any analysis of incomes and poverty for this group. However, low-paid workers may have a higher or lower household income, according to four main factors in their lives:

1   *Hours of work.* A low-paid worker may increase income from work by taking a second job and/or working longer hours and overtime. Thus, an individual might have very low hourly wages but an adequate weekly income by means of working very long hours each week.

2   *Other sources of market income.* In some cases, the earnings of an individual employee may be supplemented by other sources of market income, such as self-employment income or unearned income from an occupational pension.

3   *Income of other people that contribute to household income.* Households often consist of more than one earner – a couple with both in work, for example, or a group of young adults sharing a house. Even if others in a household are not employees, they may still have self-employment or investment income that will affect whether household income is above the poverty line. Some people may also have access to regular additional income from people outside the household, through child support payments, for example.

4   *State transfers: benefits and tax credits.* Income from work can be supplemented by claiming social security benefits and tax credits, including universal transfers such as child benefit and means-tested support such as housing benefit.

These are not mutually exclusive categories, of course, and different people will be able to combine these options in various different ways. Young people do not have much access to state transfers but many do live with their parents. Married men with young children may have non-employed wives but tend to work longer than average weekly hours. Lone mothers do not have access to a working partner and may not be able to work long hours, but many are eligible for state transfers and some get regular child support payments from a former partner. The actual extent of income sharing within the household will also affect whether individuals are living in poverty or not (this is discussed in more detail in Chapter 3). Hence, the poverty-avoidance strategies people can opt for are determined by a number of factors including benefit rules, personal preferences and, to a large extent, where the individual is in the life cycle, since this will influence their labour market opportunities and family circumstances. What we observe people do in practice will reflect their personal response to these factors and also to the trade-off between their need to avoid poverty and other needs, such as spending time with their family or investing in their education.

These strategies affecting household income are a mixture of the individual (e.g. working overtime to boost your own wages) and the relational (e.g. living with a partner who is also in paid work). Current policy is also structured with a mixture of individual and family-based measures. There are various provisions intended to support incomes in work but the two most important elements in the current policy mix are the national minimum wage and the system of tax credits, both introduced in 1999. (See later chapters for further discussion of how these work.) The national minimum wage sets the minimum level of *individual gross hourly wages*; the tax credits are assessed according to *family gross annual income*. These measures are thus targeted on different units (individual and family), relate to different time periods (hourly and annually), and may be received by different family members (wages are received by individual workers, tax credits are paid to both the main earner and the main carer), over different time periods (weekly, monthly or in lump-sum payments).

These differences in targeting reflect the fact that there are two, complementary but different, policy objectives here. One is to increase low wages for individual workers and the other is to increase the incomes of low-income working families.[1] Low wages are an individual attribute, and not all low-wage workers live in low-income households. Low-income households may, or may not, include low-paid workers. The two sets of provision are therefore targeted differently but they are also intended to work together. The logic is that the minimum wage sets a floor for hourly gross pay while tax credits top this up to provide an adequate level of weekly income taking account of family size and/or disability. The Treasury describes this as providing 'guaranteed minimum incomes for working households in a variety of circumstances' (Balls *et al.*, 2004, p. 223), although this is a guarantee that depends on the number of hours of paid work as well as on family composition, disability status and the take-up of tax credits.

The aim of this research is to explore the relationship between individual low pay, hours of work, other sources of household income, benefits and tax credits and household poverty. The starting point in Chapter 2 is individual hourly low pay. Using data from the Family Expenditure Survey (Office for National Statistics, 2002), we examine the extent and risk of low pay – defined as hourly gross pay below two-thirds of the median – in Britain from the mid-1990s to 2000/1. According to our estimates, about 5.4 million employees were low-paid in 2000/1, almost a quarter of the employed workforce. Thus, low pay remains a significant issue, affecting many people. We then go on in Chapter 3 to examine the household incomes of individual low-paid people and the contribution made by the various different sources of income to poverty avoidance.

This study is, to some extent, a repeat, six years on, of a previous analysis using the same data set and a similar analytical approach (Webb *et al.*, 1996; Millar *et al.*, 1997).

We are thus able to set this analysis in a longer time period as well as to compare the situation of low-paid workers in the mid-1990s (just before the election of the Labour government) and in the early 2000s (after the introduction of the national minimum wage and the first generation of tax credits). In the remainder of this report, we describe the nature and objectives of the key policy instruments alongside the data analysis, and conclude with a discussion of current policy issues and future options in Chapter 4.

2 Low hourly pay: incidence, trends and characteristics

Low hourly pay is associated with particular jobs and industries. The jobs at the bottom of the pay ladder include cleaning, catering, care work, sales, security and hairdressing. The industries where low pay is concentrated include textiles, agriculture, hotels and catering, retail, and residential care (McKnight, 2002). These jobs and sectors are often female-dominated and many low-paid jobs are held by women, especially women working part-time. When the national minimum wage was introduced in 1999, as many as three-quarters of those who benefited were women (Dickens and Manning, 2003). Young people just entering the labour force are also more likely to be low-paid than older workers, particularly if they are paid as trainees (Low Pay Commission, 2004). But low pay is not confined just to women and young people, as our previous research on trends in low pay between the late 1960s and the mid-1990s showed (Webb *et al.*, 1996; Millar *et al.*, 1997). Our two key findings were, first, that low pay has become more widespread and is affecting more people, including men and older workers; and, second, that the overlap between low pay and poverty has increased because more low-paid workers are either living alone or have responsibility for dependants (see also Stewart, 1999). This chapter explores the first of these points and examines the extent of low pay in the UK, the risk of low pay by gender, age and family type, and the concentration of low pay in families. We also look at the relationship between low hourly pay and low weekly earnings in order to see whether some low-paid people are working their way out of low earnings by putting in long hours of work each week. Chapter 3 then addresses the relationship between low pay and poverty.

Data and definitions

The analysis is based on the Family Expenditure Survey,[1] which provides detailed information on incomes and expenditure for individuals and households across the UK.[2] The sample we use for this study consists of individuals who are employees, aged 16 and over, either currently at work or temporarily absent, and for whom the necessary wages data are available. This produces a sample of around 5,700 people in each year (varying slightly from year to year). The analysis focuses on 2000/1, and looks at comparisons over time from 1994/5 to 2000/1, with a year running from April to March.

There are various points to note about this sample and these definitions. First, the Family Expenditure Survey is a sample of private households, which means it is unlikely to pick up some groups of potentially low-paid workers, for example migrant workers, travellers and homeless people.

Second, the focus is only on employees, excluding self-employed people for whom earnings data are much less reliable. Some self-employed people have very low earnings and a high risk of poverty, with 22 per cent of self-employed people living in poor households in 2000/1 (DWP, 2003a). Although the self-employment rate has declined over time (Weir, 2003), the classification of people as 'self-employed' rather than 'employee' may be a somewhat arbitrary distinction.

These exclusions mean that the Family Expenditure Survey cannot provide a complete picture of low earnings in the UK. However, our definition of an employee is designed to be as inclusive as possible. We include all those who define their primary economic status as 'employee' regardless of hours of work, so we include those with very short, as well as those with very long, weekly hours. We also include all age groups, not just people of 'working age'. Among young people this means we include a small number who are still in education but who are at the same time also employees working for pay. Among older people we similarly include those past retirement age but who are still employees working for pay. This gives a very comprehensive coverage of the employed workforce and means that we are not excluding some groups of employees who might have a high risk of low hourly pay just because they are not working very many hours each week. Given our inclusive definition of the low-paid population, it could be argued that when we look at the ability to avoid poverty one would not expect the market income of the very young or very old to be sufficient to enable their households to avoid poverty. However, this does not justify excluding such individuals from a study of low pay, and even in our analysis of the ability to avoid poverty, it does not seem valid to make an *a priori* judgement that these employees are less able to contribute to household income than other employees in the household.

Low pay can be defined in various ways, but the most common definitions are based on hourly gross pay in relation to the median. Hourly wages are chosen in preference to weekly earnings because hourly pay is a better measure of reward for a fixed period of work, not varying with the number of hours worked. (Weekly earnings are a better measure of the level of living standards achieved through paid work.) Gross wages are similarly a better measure of reward for work than net wages, since net wages depend on the structure and level of deductions from gross pay that vary for different people. The low pay threshold can be defined as those at the bottom of the earnings distribution – the lowest 10 or 20 per cent, for example – but relating pay to the median gives a better measure of how low pay relates to the earnings distribution as a whole. The low pay threshold used here is gross hourly pay of less than two-thirds of the median for all employees in the UK aged 16 years and above. When adopting a relative definition of low pay, the precise cut-off will always be an arbitrary choice but this is the measure used in our previous study analysis, providing a time series on low pay back to 1968, and is in line with recent studies of low pay (for example, see McKnight, 2002). More information on the calculation of hourly pay is provided in the discussion of data and definitions in the Appendix.

It should be noted that this definition of low pay is higher than the level of the national minimum wage. In 1999, when the national minimum wage was introduced, it was set at a level of £3.60 per hour.[3] Our low hourly pay threshold was £4.69 at that time. Similarly, in 2000/1 the national minimum wage rate was £3.70 (rising to £4.10 in October 2001) and our low pay threshold was £4.86. The national minimum wage thus does not affect the overall extent of low hourly wages, when low pay is defined as below two-thirds of the median (see further discussion below).

The incidence of low pay in the UK

Table 1 shows that, according to our estimates, in 2000/1 around 5.4 million workers, or around 23 per cent of all UK employees, were low-paid according to this definition of hourly gross pay below two-thirds of the median. This includes 2.1 million men, or just over 17 per cent of all male workers, and 3.2 million women, or just under 30 per cent of all female workers. Almost equal numbers of full-time and part-time workers (taking a 30 hours cut-off) were low-paid – 2.9 and 2.5 million respectively – but this amounts to 16 per cent of full-time workers compared with 48 per cent of part-time workers. The average hourly pay of all low-paid employees was about £3.67 gross, £3.72 for full-time and £3.60 for part-time employees.

Table 1   Low pay, all employees: UK, 2000/1

	All	Full-time employees[a]	Part-time employees[b]
Low pay threshold (hourly)	£4.86	£4.86	£4.86
Mean hourly pay of low-paid employees	£3.67	£3.72	£3.60
Number of low-paid employees (million)	5.4	2.9	2.5
% of all employees who are low-paid	23.2	16.0	48.2
Number of low-paid men employees (million)	2.1	1.5	0.6
% of men employees who are low-paid	17.5	13.6	58.0
Number of low-paid women employees (million)	3.2	1.3	1.9
% of women employees who are low-paid	29.6	19.8	45.7

Source: Here and in other tables, own analyses of the Family Expenditure Survey.
a   30 hours and above.
b   Under 30 hours.

Table 2 shows the incidence of low hourly pay among men and women by family type and age. People under 22 and single people have the highest rates of low pay (these two groups overlap substantially, of course), and young or single men are just as likely to be low-paid as young or single women. But there are clear differences between men and women in other age groups, with 24 per cent of women aged 22–49 being low-paid compared with 11 per cent of men in the same age range, and 29 per cent of women aged over 50 compared with 12 per cent of men. And women in couples or who are lone parents have a much greater risk of low pay than men in the same family situation.

Table 2   Incidence of low hourly pay by gender, age and family type, 2000/1

	Men	Women	All	Unweighted base
	(% low-paid in each category)			
All	18	30	23	(5,673)
Age				
Under 18	82	81	81	(138)
18–21	65	65	65	(368)
22–49	11	24	17	(3,902)
50 plus	12	29	20	(1,265)
Family type				
Single, no children	33	35	34	(1,531)
Single with children	7	27	25	(207)
Couple, no children	10	26	18	(1,890)
Couple with children	9	29	18	(2,045)

Trends in low pay over time

Table 3 shows the proportion of employees with hourly low wages each year from 1994/5 to 2000/1. The low pay threshold rises from £3.84 per hour in 1994/5 to £4.86 in 2000/1, reflecting the rise in wages over that period. Overall, the proportion defined as low-paid has stayed stable over this period at around 23 per cent of those in employment. There is a clear difference between men and women in these trends. For employed men, the proportion with low pay *rises* from 13.8 per cent in the mid-1990s to 17.5 per cent at the end; for employed women it *falls* from 32.9 to 29.6 per cent. The relative risk of low pay for women compared with men thus falls sharply from 2.4 in 1994/5 to 1.7 in 2000/1.[4]

Figure 1 takes a longer look back to the late 1960s and shows that for most of the period around 20–23 per cent of employees had low hourly wages, apart from a fall in the late 1970s. However, this disguises the rather different trends for men and women over the past 30 or so years. Among men, the proportion with low hourly wages was stable at around 8 per cent through the 1970s before rising to around 14 per cent by the mid-1990s and to just over 17 per cent by 2000/1. For women the

Table 3   Hourly low pay, 1994/5 to 2000/1

	Hourly low pay threshold	% all low-paid	% men low-paid	% women low-paid	Relative risk women/men
1994/5	£3.84	23.0	13.8	32.9	2.4
1995/6	£3.95	22.6	14.4	31.6	2.2
1996/7	£4.13	23.3	14.5	32.7	2.3
1997/8	£4.30	23.5	16.3	31.6	1.9
1998/9	£4.39	22.9	15.2	31.6	2.1
1999/0	£4.69	23.7	15.6	32.7	2.1
2000/1	£4.86	23.2	17.5	29.6	1.7

proportion who were low-paid fell sharply between 1968 and 1977, from around 48 per cent to 30 per cent. This dip probably reflects the impact of government wages policy at that time, which was aimed at reducing pay differentials, and the equal pay legislation of the mid-1970s. The proportion with low wages then rose slightly and stabilised at around 32–34 per cent for the 1980s and into the 1990s, falling to just under 30 per cent in the last year for which we have data.[5]

Over this time period, the level of participation of men and women in the labour market has changed. The number of men in employment has fallen while the number of women has risen. Therefore, these changes in the *rates* of low pay have different outcomes in respect of *numbers.* For men the rate of low pay has risen and so have the numbers of low-paid men, as low-paid men are now a larger proportion of a smaller number. In 1968, our estimates show that in total there were just under 14 million male employees; by 2000/1 this had fallen to about 12 million. The number of low-paid men nearly doubled over that period from just over one to just over two million.

Figure 1   Proportion of hourly low-paid employees by sex, 1968 to 2000/1

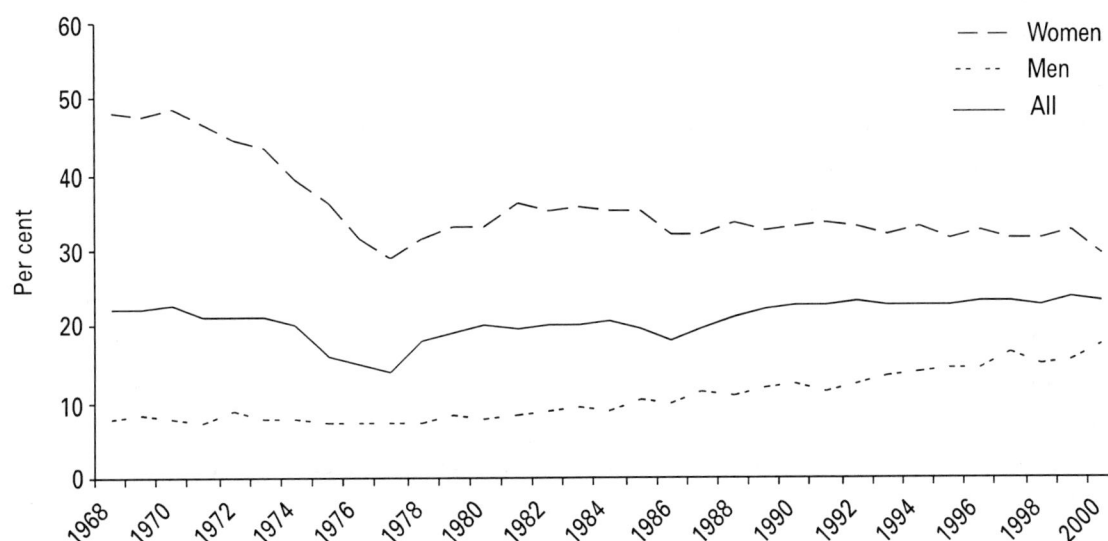

Among women, the rates have fallen steeply but the numbers have only fallen a little, as low-paid women are now a smaller proportion of a larger number. The number of women in employment rose from just under eight million in 1968 to about 11 million in 2000/1. The number of low-paid women was about 3.7 million in 1968 and about 3.2 million in 2000/1. Thus, the numbers of low-paid men and women have tended to converge. Women still outnumber men among the low-paid by about three to two. But in the late 1960s there were six low-paid women for every low-paid man.

In our previous study, we concluded that 'twenty-five years ago the stereotypical low-paid worker would be either a young single person or a married woman. Today, although low-paid employees are still most likely to be female, men make up almost one-third of low-paid employees … among men in particular there has been a dramatic increase in the proportion of low-paid employees who are in the 25–49 age group' (Millar *et al.*, 1997, p. 12; see also Stewart, 1999). Taking the story into the twenty-first century confirms these points:

- In 1968 and in 2000/1 about *23 per cent of all employees* were low-paid. In 1968 this was about *4.8 million* people, in 2000/1 it was about *5.4 million* people.

- About 8 per cent of *male employees* were low-paid in 1968 – 1.1 million men. In 2000/1, about 18 per cent of male employees were low-paid – 2.2 million men.

- About 48 per cent of *female employees* were low-paid in 1968 – 3.7 million women. In 2000/1, about 30 per cent of female employees were low-paid – 3.2 million women.

In 2000/1, about 0.7 million low-paid men and 1.7 million low-paid women were aged between 25 and 49. Low pay has increasingly become an issue for people – men and women – who may be supporting families, rather than young people just starting out on their working lives. The development of in-work cash transfers over this period, from family income supplement in the early 1970s through family credit in the mid-1980s to tax credits in the late 1990s, thus reflects a growing need for wage supplementation among a wider range of people.

The impact of the national minimum wage

As noted above, our low pay threshold of two-thirds of median gross hourly pay is higher than the level of the national minimum wage. We would therefore not expect to see any impact on low pay overall, although we would expect the number earning below the national minimum wage level to fall. We did find some evidence for this, with a reduction in the proportion earning below the level of the national minimum wage introduced in April 1999 from 8.8 per cent in 1998/9 to 5.8 per cent in 1999/2000. This suggests that some people were still earning below the national minimum wage level after its introduction in 1999. There are two main explanations for this.

First, it may reflect non-compliance with the national minimum wage legislation. Although compliance has generally been high (Low Pay Commission, 2004), there is a variety of evidence that substantial numbers of individuals continue to be paid below the national minimum wage level. Heasman (2003), for example, finds that there was a sharp drop in the number of jobs paid below the national minimum wage level between 1999 and 2000, suggesting some delay in response to the legislation. National Statistics (2003) was still showing about 260,000 jobs paying below national minimum wage levels by spring 2003. Second, as highlighted in our discussion of how to estimate hourly wages (see Appendix), there have been some problems in assessing the impact of the national minimum wage because of the lack of adequate and reliable data.

In general, the evidence suggests that the effect of the national minimum wage has been less than was expected. The main initial impact was to move people from below the level of the national minimum wage level to exactly this level, or just above, and there has been little or no effect on the pay of other employees (Metcalf, 2002). Dickens and Manning (2003, p. 201) conclude that 'at most 3.7 per cent (815,000) of adult workers received a pay rise' when the national minimum wage was introduced, three-quarters of these being women. Sutherland (2001) shows that the national minimum wage had little impact on poverty. There have been calls for the level of the national minimum wage to be increased, and the government has accepted the recommendation of the Low Pay Commission (2004) suggesting a rate of £4.85 from October 2004, with the aim of covering about 1.7 million workers.[6]

Low hourly pay, family and household type

Table 4 compares the gender, age and family type of hourly low-paid employees with other employees who are not low-paid. As discussed above, the risk of low pay is highest for women, for young people and for single people. This is also reflected in the characteristics of the low-paid group, who are more likely than other employees to be female, young or single. But it should also be noted that people aged 22 to 49 make up about half of the low-paid population, that couples make up just over half (52 per cent) and that people with children make up about a third (31 per cent). So many low-paid employees do have responsibility for dependants.

Table 4   Characteristics of hourly low-paid and non-low-paid employees, 2000/1

	Hourly low-paid (%)	Not hourly low-paid (%)
Men	40	57
Women	60	43
Aged under 18	10	1
Aged 18–21	21	3
Aged 22–49	50	74
Aged 50 plus	18	22
Mean age	(33.5)	(39.5)
Single, no children	45	27
Single with children	4	3
Couple, no children	25	34
Couple with children	27	36
Unweighted base	(1,274)	(4,399)

In the analysis so far we have compared the extent and risk of low pay by the type of 'family' in which the low-paid person lives. Here a family is defined in the same way as the unit used for tax and benefit calculations – that is, adults and dependent children (single, single with dependent children, couple and couple with dependent children). Dependent children are aged under 16 or under 19 and in full-time education. But it is also revealing to consider the wider household in which these family units are based. The definition of a household is a person or people who live at the same address and share meals, living accommodation or common housekeeping (see Box 1 below for further details). Hence, people may live in households that are larger than just their family: for example, non-dependent children living with their parents, or people sharing with other non-related adults. So, one or more individuals make up a family and one or more families make up a household.

While the definition of the household used here is standard, definitions of a family unit may vary. For example, in both the General Household Survey and the Labour Force Survey, a family is defined to include non-dependent children, if those children are never married and childless. We define such adult children as a separate family unit within the household, which means we can identify each financially (for tax and benefit purposes) distinct unit within the household. This is important for the analysis of household poverty that follows (in Chapter 3). The Appendix provides a detailed verification of these results for people living in multiple-family households with those from other surveys.

Overall, about a third (34 per cent) of our full sample of employees were living in households that included people other than their own family (benefit) unit. Low-paid employees are even more likely to live in households with other families. As Table 5 shows, over half – 53 per cent – of the low-paid employees were sharing with others in 2000/1. This difference is mainly accounted for by the higher proportion among the low-paid employees who are living with parents (20 per cent compared with 9 per cent of all employees). This is especially the case for the low-paid single people, of whom only 15 per cent live alone while 41 per cent live with their parents and 31 per cent live with a mixture of other people (parents and/or grown-up children and/or other adults). This is quite different from all single employees, of whom 40 per cent live alone, 27 per cent live with parents only and 18 per cent live in mixed households.

Table 5 shows that about 28 per cent of all employed lone parents are living in households with other adults, and lone parents who are low-paid are even more likely to live with others (36 per cent). Those who live with others most commonly live with their adult children. About 22 per cent of the low-paid lone parents live with their non-dependent children only, about 10 per cent live with their parents only and about 4 per cent live in other more complex households.

Table 5   Household structure by family type: all employees and low-paid employees, 2000/1 (%)

	Single, no children	Single, with children	Couple, no children	Couple, with children	All
All employees					
No other adults[a]	40	72	75	81	66
Non-dependent children only	3	19	20	16	13
Parents only	27	5	1	1	9
Other only[b]	12	1	3	2	5
Mixed[c]	18	2	1	1	6
Unweighted base	(1,531)	(207)	(1,890)	(2,045)	(5,673)
Low-paid employees					
No other adults[a]	15	64	70	78	47
Non-dependent children only	2	22	24	17	12
Parents only	41	10	3	2	20
Other only[b]	10	0	2	2	5
Mixed[c]	31	4	1	1	15
Unweighted base	(509)	(51)	(344)	(370)	(1,274)

a   Apart from individual and partner, where there is a partner.
b   Neither children nor parents, e.g. sibling, grandparent or friend.
c   Live with adults who are a mixture of non-dependent children, parents and other.

By contrast, among couples, both with and without dependent children, there is very little difference in household arrangements between the low-paid employees and employees in general. These families are the family type most likely to live alone and, if they do not live alone, to live with only non-dependent children.

Thus, over half of all low-paid employees live in households where there is at least the potential for more than one earner. In Chapter 3 we consider the implications of this for household poverty. Table 6 focuses just on couples in order to examine whether there is any relationship between employment position among both partners in couples. This shows that low-paid employees are more likely than those who are not low-paid to have a non-employed partner (35 per cent compared with 28 per cent), although both groups are equally likely to have a low-paid partner (12 per cent). Low-paid men are more likely than other men to have a non-employed partner (42 per cent compared with 30 per cent) and are also more likely to have a low-paid partner (23 per cent compared with 17 per cent). The same is true for low-paid women (32 per cent with a non-employed partner compared with 25 per cent; 8 per cent with a low-paid partner compared with 5 per cent). So, four in ten low-paid men in couples are the sole earners for their families, as are three in ten low-paid women.

Low hourly pay, working hours and weekly earnings

So far we have been looking at hourly low pay but, as discussed in the Introduction, we are also interested in poverty and living standards and so we need to consider what sort of weekly earnings these hourly wages generate. As Table 7 shows, hourly low pay is more common among those who work shorter weekly hours in their main

Table 6   Low hourly pay among couples, 2000/1

	Hourly low-paid (%)	Not hourly low-paid (%)
Partners		
Not employed	35	28
Employed – low-paid	12	12
Employed – not low-paid	54	61
Partners of men		
Not employed	42	30
Employed – low-paid	23	17
Employed – not low-paid	36	53
Partners of women		
Not employed	32	25
Employed – low-paid	8	5
Employed – not low-paid	60	71
Unweighted base	(712)	(3,199)

Table 7   Incidence of hourly low pay by weekly hours in main job, 2000/1

	Men	Women	All
	(% low hourly paid in each category)		
Under 16 hours	61	55	56
16–23 hours	61	41	44
24–34 hours	19	26	24
35 hours plus	14	20	16
Unweighted base	(443)	(831)	(1,274)

job – 56 per cent of those working for less than 16 hours per week (the tax credits cut-off) are low-paid compared with 16 per cent of those working 35 hours plus. Men working fewer weekly hours are particularly likely to be low-paid.

Table 8 compares hours in main job and earnings, for low-paid and non-low-paid employees. Those who are not low-paid are rarely in main jobs with very short hours: just 5 per cent work for under 16 hours per week compared with 21 per cent of the low-paid, and 72 per cent work for 35-plus hours per week compared with 44 per cent of the low-paid. The mean weekly hours are 37.5 and 30.5 respectively. The mean hourly wages of the hourly low-paid are £3.67, about £1.20 below the low pay threshold. The mean hourly wages of those not hourly low-paid are around £10.98, more than double the low pay threshold. The weekly earnings of the non-low-paid are more than three times as high as those of the low-paid (£405 and £115), reflecting both their longer hours and their higher hourly rates of pay.

Thus, hourly low pay does, for many employees, also translate into low weekly earnings, which suggests that low-paid people are likely to be at an increased risk of poverty, especially for those who are reliant only upon their own wages.

Table 8   Hours in main job and pay: low-paid and non-low-paid employees, 2000/1

	Hourly low-paid	Not hourly low-paid
Working under 16 hours	21%	5%
16–23 hours	16%	6%
24–34 hours	18%	17%
35 hours plus	44%	72%
Mean hours – main job	30.5	37.5
Mean hourly wages	£3.67	£10.89
Mean hourly pay gap/surplus	–£1.20	+£6.03
Mean weekly earnings	£115.24	£405.69
Unweighted base	(1,274)	(4,399)

Weekly low pay

As we have seen above, on average, those who are hourly low-paid are also likely to work shorter hours in their main job and therefore also have low weekly earnings. But some people with hourly low earnings may be able to boost their weekly earnings by second jobs and/or by working long hours. The extent of second jobs is limited, although more often found among those who are hourly low-paid (4 per cent with at least one subsidiary job) than among those who are not hourly low-paid (2 per cent). In order to start to explore the relationship between low pay and living standards, here we examine the relationship between *low hourly pay* and *low weekly earnings* for individual employees. We have defined the latter in the same way as low hourly pay, that is, earning below two-thirds of the weekly median. In 2000/1 this means a low weekly earnings threshold of £188 per week.

On this basis, weekly low earnings are more common than hourly low wages, with 30 per cent of the sample being weekly low-paid, compared with the 23 per cent who are hourly low-paid. We would perhaps expect this greater variability in weekly earnings, since differences arise due to variation both in hourly wages and in hours worked. Women are much more likely to be weekly low-paid than men – 45 per cent compared with 14 per cent. In general, the characteristics associated with weekly low earnings are similar to those associated with hourly low wages – women, young people, single people and those working fewer hours are most at risk.

Table 9 shows that those who are hourly low-paid are usually also weekly low-paid (87 per cent), while those who are not low-paid on an hourly basis are usually not low-paid weekly either (88 per cent). The patterns are rather different for men and women. Among hourly low-paid men there is a substantial minority – about a quarter – who are not low-paid on a weekly basis. These men must be working long hours each week. Very few (6 per cent) hourly low-paid women manage this. Among the women, however, about a quarter of those who are not hourly low-paid are low-paid on a weekly basis. These women must be working quite short hours but in relatively well-paid jobs.

Thus, as Table 10 shows, about 67 per cent of all employees are not low-paid on either the hourly or the weekly basis. These are more likely to be men than women, their mean hourly pay is about £11, and their mean hours per week are about 40, including two hours of overtime. Their average weekly earnings are almost £450. Their situation contrasts sharply with that of the 20 per cent who are low-paid on both an hourly and a weekly basis. Hourly pay for this group is around £3.50, weekly

Table 9   Hourly by weekly low pay, 2000/1

	Hourly low-paid (%)	Not hourly low-paid (%)
All		
Weekly low-paid	87	12
Not weekly low-paid	13	88
Men		
Weekly low-paid	76	3
Not weekly low-paid	24	97
Women		
Weekly low-paid	94	24
Not weekly low-paid	6	76
Unweighted base	(1,274)	(4,399)

hours are around 27 (with very little overtime compared with other groups) and weekly pay is under £100. Those who are hourly low-paid only are quite a small group – just 3 per cent of all employees – and mainly men. They have mean hourly earnings of around £4.20 but they work very long hours in their main jobs (over 52 hours per week on average including overtime) and are the most likely to have subsidiary jobs as well. This takes their weekly earnings to about £230. The final group (9 per cent of all employees) are low-paid only on a weekly basis. Their average hours are around 19 per week, enough to give them weekly earnings above those of the hourly low-paid group, despite their much shorter hours.

Table 10   Hourly and weekly low pay by gender, pay and hours, 2000/1

	Neither (67%)	Both (20%)	Hourly only (3%)	Weekly only (9%)
Men	63%	35%	72%	16%
Women	37%	65%	28%	84%
Mean hourly pay – main job	£11.41	£3.57	£4.27	£7.19
Mean weekly hours – main job, overtime	2.2	1.4	7.0	0.6
Mean weekly hours – main job, total	40.1	27.2	52.4	18.8
Percentage with a subsidiary job	2%	4%	9%	4%
Mean weekly pay – subsidiary jobs	£2.12	£1.29	£8.38	£1.38
Mean weekly pay – main job	£442.69	£96.00	£221.32	£118.44
Mean weekly pay – all jobs	£445.49	£97.68	£230.34	£120.15
Unweighted base	(3,850)	(1,106)	(168)	(549)

Summary

This analysis of the Family Expenditure Survey shows that about 5.4 million employees in the UK are low-paid, in that they are earning less than two-thirds of the hourly gross median for all employees. The low pay threshold used here is higher than the level of the national minimum wage. Those most at risk of low pay are women, young people and single people. Low pay is rising among men, in respect of both the proportion and the number. For women, the proportion who are low-paid has been falling, but the number has changed very little.

Although young people have the highest risk of low pay, the vast majority (69 per cent) of hourly low-paid employees are aged over 21 and about a third have dependent children. In addition, low-paid employees are more likely than others to be living with other adults in their household. This is especially true of single low-paid people, many of whom live with parents, and of lone parents who live with non-dependent children. Many low-paid men have non-working, or low-paid, partners. This is also true, but to a lesser extent, for women. About four in ten low-paid men in couples are the sole earners for their families, as are three in ten low-paid women in couples.

Those who are low-paid on an hourly basis tend to work for fewer hours per week, so they also have low weekly earnings. There is a substantial degree of overlap between low hourly pay and low weekly earnings. Most women who are low-paid on an hourly basis also have low weekly earnings. Men with low hourly pay can sometimes avoid low weekly earnings by very long hours of work. Thus, we can begin to see how low hourly pay relates to low weekly earnings and to raise questions about the contribution of other family and household members to income. The next chapter explores these issues more fully.

3 Avoiding poverty: household resources and state transfers

Paid work reduces the risk of poverty but does not eliminate it. As other researchers have shown, those who have jobs, or those children whose parents have jobs, have lower rates of poverty than those who do not. Working full-time is better than working part-time for avoiding poverty, and so is having more than one worker in the family. The official Households Below Average Income series shows this clearly (DWP, 2003, Table 5.7). In 2000/1, about 14 per cent of the working-age population were living in poor households: that is, households with net equivalent incomes before housing costs of less than 60 per cent of the median. The risk of poverty varied significantly by work status – from 2 per cent of single people or two-earner couples working full-time, to 3 per cent of two-earner (one full-time and one part-time) couples, to 11 per cent of one-earner couples, to 24 per cent of those in households with one or more part-time workers. By contrast, 60 per cent of those living in unemployed households were living in poor households. However, although households with workers have a lower risk of poverty than non-working households, they still make up a substantial proportion of all those in poverty. About half of poor working-age adults lived in households that included one or more people in paid work (including the self-employed), and almost half of children living in poverty were living in households with one or more workers (DWP, 2003).[1]

Low-paid workers are, not surprisingly, more at risk of living in poverty than other workers and acutely so if they are the only worker in their household. McKnight (2002) calculates that, in 1996, 53 per cent of households with just one, low-paid, worker (defined as in the lowest quintile) were living in poverty (defined in that study as below half the median after housing costs) compared with 16 per cent of households with one worker who is higher-paid, and just 2 per cent with two higher-paid workers. She also makes comparisons between 1968 and 1996 and shows that the proportion of households with just one low-paid worker increased from 1 per cent to 3 per cent, and their risk of poverty increased from 24 per cent to 53 per cent. Low-paid workers have become both more numerous and more prone to poverty. Sutherland *et al.* (2003) show that 16 per cent of low-paid workers were living in poor households in 2000/1 compared with 5 per cent of workers in general (this analysis, however, used a threshold of 60 per cent median for both hourly wages and income, whereas here we use two-thirds and 60 per cent respectively). Looking at the dynamics of low pay and poverty, Stewart (1999) finds that people who were low-paid continuously over a four-year period were five times as likely to be living in poor households as those who were never low-paid during this period.

In this chapter we explore the overlap between low pay and poverty in order to examine the extent to which low-paid employees are living in poor households. What has not been examined in other studies is the contribution of different individuals and sources of income to total household income in order to explore how it is that most low-paid people manage to avoid household poverty. Can they do this by just their earnings alone? Or do they need to have access to other sources of income, and, if so, what? Going inside the household in this way allows us to build up a picture of the way in which earnings, income from other household members and benefits and tax credits help people to avoid poverty.

Low pay and poverty

The starting point for this analysis is to calculate household income and estimate the number of individuals living in poor households. We have measured household income in a way that is as close as possible to the Households Below Average Income (HBAI) definition. All sources of regular household income are included, net of deductions for tax and national insurance, and total income is then adjusted to take account of household size and composition.[2] Poor households are households with total incomes below 60 per cent of median equivalised disposable household income, before housing costs. Box 1 discusses some of the implications of this definition for our analysis of low pay and household poverty.

Box 1   Issues in household poverty measurement

Households are defined as a single person or group of people living at the same address, which is their main residence, and who share meals or living accommodation or have common housekeeping.[3] This is not the same as a family or tax/benefit unit, which is defined as a single adult or a couple, plus any dependent children (children aged under 16 or under 19 and in full-time education). So a household may contain more than one 'family' even if it only consists of parents with dependent and non-dependent children, since the latter form a separate family/benefit unit.

As with the HBAI, we are using a household measure of poverty, in which all income coming into the household is assumed to be equally available to all members of that household. If the household is poor then everyone in the household is counted as poor; if the household is not poor than no one in the household is counted as poor. This assumption about equal income sharing is a standard aspect of poverty measurement that is based on household (or family) units, rather than on individuals, because most surveys of household income do not collect information on how income spending is allocated within the household or family. Specific studies of access to income within these units show that income is not always shared in this way (Vogler and Pahl, 1993; Goode *et al.*, 1998; Rake and Jayatilaka, 2002).

In particular, it may be that income sharing within the household is a more realistic assumption for some household types than others. For example, single-family households may be more likely to pool more of their income than multi-family households. Young adults may be more likely to benefit from living with their parents than with non-related people.

For this analysis we separately identify the relative contributions of different components of household income and of different individuals to household poverty avoidance. This shows whether people can, as individual earners, support themselves and the people they live with or whether they can only do so with contributions from others. Thus, it also provides a way of examining the contribution of both men and women to the avoidance of poverty within the household, highlighting interdependency between men and women rather than assuming that women are financially dependent on men (Millar, 2003).

Also in common with HBAI, we are using a static definition of poverty measured on the basis of income data for one point in time. Results for different years can then be compared to give a picture of trends over time. But the dynamics of poverty avoidance for particular individuals is not explored here.

The poverty definition used here is a *before housing costs* measure. Housing costs are, of course, an important determinant of living standards since they represent a relatively 'fixed cost' for most individuals, at least in the short run. Those households with more expensive housing would be more likely to be identified as poor using an after housing costs poverty definition. However, in the context of this study it is more appropriate to analyse poverty before housing costs have been deducted from income. The framework used here requires a breakdown of how separate sources of income and different individuals within the household contribute to total household income. It is not clear how housing costs should be treated within this framework, since we would have to make assumptions about how this expenditure is shared within the household. We would prefer to make as few assumptions of this kind as possible for the reasons discussed above. An additional reason to use a before housing costs measure is that it is the measure that has been adopted by the government as one of the three indicators (absolute low income, relative low income and material deprivation) of child poverty (DWP, 2003a).

As Table 11 shows, we estimate that about 20 per cent of all individuals – adults and children – live in poor households. This is slightly higher than the HBAI estimate of 17 per cent in 2000/1 (DWP, 2003, Table D6.1), with the disparity accounted for by some differences in the data and definitions (see Appendix for details and further comparisons with HBAI). As expected, employed people have a much lower risk of living in poverty than people in general, with 5 per cent of employees living in poor households compared with 20 per cent of all individuals and 19 per cent of all adults. Those who are hourly low-paid are more likely to be living in household poverty than other employees (14 per cent compared with 2 per cent). Low-paid men have a higher risk of household poverty than low-paid women (17 per cent compared with 13 per cent).

Thus, the vast majority of hourly low-paid people – 86 per cent – do not live in poor households. However, the overlap between low pay and poverty is much higher now than used to be the case. In our previous study we found that the overlap between low pay and household poverty was about 3 to 4 per cent of all low-paid employees in the 1970s and 1980s but had started to increase by the late 1980s (Webb *et al.*, 1996) and had tripled by 1994/5. Table 12 compares the situation in 1994/5 and 2000/1. This shows that the proportion of *all employees* living in household poverty has remained about the same over that period, at 4 per cent in 1994/5 and 5 per cent in 2000/1. For low-paid employees, the overlap between low pay and poverty has increased slightly from 11 to 14 per cent.[4] There is some variation in this by gender and family type.

Table 11   Low hourly pay and household poverty, 2000/1

	Household poor (%)	Non-household poor (%)	Unweighted base
All individuals	20	80	(15,925)
All adults	19	81	(11,921)
All employees	5	95	(5,673)
Low-paid employees	14	86	(1,274)
Non-low-paid employees	2	98	(4,399)
Men employees	5	95	(2,828)
Low-paid	17	83	(443)
Non-low-paid	2	98	(2,385)
Women employees	6	94	(2,845)
Low-paid	13	87	(831)
Non-low-paid	3	97	(2,014)

For low-paid employed men, the risk of household poverty has risen from 10 per cent in 1994/5 to 17 per cent in 2000/1. The risk of poverty has risen for low-paid single men (from 5 to 14 per cent) and men in couples without children (from 3 to 11 per cent), but stayed the same for men with dependent children (at 37 per cent in both years). Thus although low-paid men with children have much the highest risk of poverty of any family type, this has not increased since the mid-1990s.

For low-paid women, the overlap between low pay and poverty rose from 11 per cent in 1994/5 to 13 per cent in 2000/1. Low-paid single women and women in couples without children are more likely to be living in household poverty in 2000/1 than their counterparts in 1994/5. For low-paid women in couples with children there has been little change, but for low-paid lone mothers the proportion living in household poverty has fallen from 28 per cent to 20 per cent.

Table 12   Low hourly pay and household poverty, 1994/5 and 2000/1

	% in household poverty	
	1994/5	2000/1
All employees	4	5
Low-paid employees	11	14
Low-paid men[a]	10	17
Single	5	14
Couple	3	11
Couple with children	37	37
Low-paid women	11	13
Single	8	14
Single with children	28	20
Couple	7	9
Couple with children	14	13
Unweighted base	(5,727)	(5,673)

a   *Numbers of lone fathers too small to show separately.*

Household income sources and household poverty

Thus, most low-paid people do not live in household poverty but those with children are more likely to do so than those without children. In order to examine how most hourly low-paid people avoid household poverty, we need to take into account the contribution of their wages alongside that of other household income. Do hourly low-paid people avoid household poverty because they live with other working people, or is it because they have access to other sources of income, or is it some combination of the two? Here we look first at the income sources coming into households and then at the contribution made by these to poverty avoidance.

Income sources

Total household income can be divided into seven main categories (see Appendix for full details):

1   own market income

2   market income of partner

3   market income of other adults in the household

4   non-means-tested social security benefits

5   tax credits

6   means-tested social security benefits

7   other household income.

Market income can thus be received by the individual concerned, by their partner, and/or by others living in the household. There are three sources of market income for each – income from earnings, income from self-employment and income from investments. People could, of course, receive income from more than one of these at the same time, so market income is the total of these three. Non-means-tested benefits have also been divided into three types – child benefit, NI pensions, and other. Tax credits are kept separate from other means-tested benefits (see Box 2 for a description and chronology of tax credits). 'Other household income' is sources of income which are not allocated to individuals in the Family Expenditure Survey and so this is a household measure. It includes various things – student top-up loans, children's income, benefits received from trade unions and any regular allowance from outside the household, including maintenance payments.

Box 2   Tax credits in the UK

In-work wage supplements have been part of the UK social security system since the early 1970s, initially through *family income supplement* and from the mid-1980s through *family credit*. Eligibility for these benefits was for most of this period confined to families with dependent children, and at first to just full-time workers but since 1992 to those working 16 or more hours per week. The amounts were determined by family size and family income measured over a five-week (or two-month) period. Once awarded, family credit payments were fixed for six months, regardless of any changes in circumstances.

In 1999, two new tax credits replaced in-work benefits: the *working families tax credit* and the *disabled person's tax credit*. These were administered by the Inland Revenue rather than the Department of Social Security (which became the Department for Work and Pensions in 2000) but otherwise had a very similar structure to family credit. Thus, like family credit, the working families tax credit was available only for families with children, it was paid to those with earnings below a certain level according to family size, there was a weekly hours threshold of 16 hours per week, and awards lasted for six months.

However, there were also some important differences. First, working families tax credit was more generous and so more families were eligible. Second, it included a 'childcare tax credit' which covered up to 70 per cent of eligible costs for registered care, subject to a maximum limit. This was also more generous than the previous childcare disregard in family credit but it was still not available to couples unless both parents were in paid work. Third, working families tax credit was paid to the main earner, through the pay packet, rather than to the main carer (as family credit had been). This was intended to reinforce work incentives, by linking the payment directly to wages. However, couples could choose to have direct payments to the carer.

The disabled person's tax credit had similar rules and rates to the working families tax credit, but was intended for people whose disability restricted their employment and so, in addition to the income test, applicants had to have been receiving an incapacity or disability benefit.

In 2003, these tax credits were abolished and replaced by the *child tax credit* and the *working tax credit*. These 'second generation' tax credits place the tax credit system even more firmly in the tax, rather than the social security, system. They are assessed on the basis of annual family taxable income in the previous tax year and stay in payment throughout the current tax year with an end-of-year reconciliation to take account of changes in income or circumstances. However, some changes in circumstances must be reported when they happen, and a new claim made, rather than at the end of the year.

The child tax credit puts all child-related payments, apart from child benefit, into one single system. Working and non-working parents are therefore both part of this integrated system. Child tax credit is paid to the main carer. The working tax credit is available to single and childless people as well as families with children, although the former have to be aged over 25 and working at least 30 hours per week (16 hours for disabled people and families with children). It includes a childcare element, which (as with working families tax credit) can meet up to 70 per cent of the costs of eligible childcare up to a maximum limit. Working tax credit was initially paid through the pay packet to the main earner for employed people, although the childcare element was paid to the main carer. In future, however, it will be paid direct rather than through the pay packet. Our analysis refers to 2000/1 when the working families tax credit was in payment. See Chapter 4 for further discussion of the new tax credits.

Table 13 shows the proportion of employees in general and of low-paid employees in receipt of these various sources of income (individuals are counted as being in receipt of a source of income where they have a weekly income of at least one pound). Since we are looking only at employees, all are receiving income from employment. Additional income from self-employment is rare, but about a quarter of all employees and a sixth of low-paid employees have income from savings (although amounts tend to be rather small). Low-paid employees are less likely than employees in general to have a partner with market income (which is most commonly earnings rather than other sources of market income). Overall, about 51 per cent of all employees have partners with market income, compared with 42 per cent of low-paid employees. However, the low-paid employees are more likely than all employees to have other kinds of income coming into the household. About half (47 per cent) live in households with other people with market income (such as parents or grown-up children), compared with 30 per cent of the non-low-paid.

Table 13 Sources of income: all employees and low-paid employees, 2000/1

	All employees	Low-paid employees
Own market income	100	100
Own net pay	100	100
Own self-employment income	1	1
Own investment income	27	16
Partner's market income	51	42
Partner's net pay	47	34
Partner's self-employment	5	5
Partner's investment income	19	13
Others' market income	30	47
Others' net pay	27	42
Others' self-employment	3	6
Others' investment	9	15
Non-means-tested benefits	53	63
Child benefit	43	49
NI pensions	7	10
Other	8	12
Tax credits	5	10
Means-tested benefits	10	17
Other sources of income in household	13	16

Two-thirds (63 per cent) have some income from non-means-tested benefits, most often child benefit, 10 per cent have some income from tax credits and 17 per cent have some income from means-tested benefits.[5] This compares with 53 per cent, 5 per cent and 10 per cent respectively for all employees. Similar proportions have income from other sources (16 per cent of the low-paid and 13 per cent of all employees). Thus, the household incomes of low-paid people are in general quite complex with a number of different sources of income contributing to the total.

Who are the others?

Thus, the household income for around half of low-paid people includes incomes from others in the household who are not part of their immediate family unit. In the previous chapter (Table 5) we showed that low-paid single people were most likely to live with parents and lone parents to live with adult non-dependent children, and that couples were the least likely to share their households with others. Table 14 compares low-paid men and low-paid women in respect of household composition. Low-paid men are less likely to live in households without other adults, apart from partners, than are low-paid women (36 per cent compared with 55 per cent). There is a substantial difference here between single men and men with partners (the number of lone fathers is too small for separate analysis). About two-fifths of single low-paid men live with their parents only and another third live in mixed households. Men in couples do not usually live with other adults, but if they do, they live with their adult children.

Table 14 Household structure by gender and family type: low-paid employees, 2000/1

	Single	Single with children[a]	Couple	Couple with children	All
Low-paid men					
No other adults[b]	14	–	73	84	36
Non-dependent children only	0	–	18	12	5
Parents only	44	–	3	1	29
Other only[c]	8	–	4	2	6
Mixed[d]	35	–	2	1	24
Unweighted base	(253)	–	(95)	(94)	(443)
Low-paid women					
No other adults[b]	18	63	69	76	55
Non-dependent children only	6	22	26	19	17
Parents only	38	11	2	2	14
Other only[c]	13	0	1	2	5
Mixed[d]	25	4	1	1	9
Unweighted base	(256)	(50)	(249)	(276)	(831)

a   Numbers of lone fathers too small to show separately.
b   Apart from individual and partner, where there is a partner.
c   Neither non-dependent children nor parents, e.g. sibling, grandparent or friend.
d   Live with adults who are a mixture of non-dependent children, parents and other.

The pattern by family type is similar for low-paid women. The single women usually live with their parents or in mixed households. The women in couples who are sharing households live with adult children. Low-paid lone mothers share with adult children (22 per cent) or with parents only (11 per cent).

Thus, any additional income that is coming into these households in which low-paid employees live with other adults is most likely to come from parents for single people and from adult children for other family types. We assume for the purposes of estimating poverty that all household income is pooled to create a total household income, regardless of the relationship between adults living together. In practice, of course, this may not always be a realistic assumption.

Avoiding poverty

In order to explore the relationship between low pay and household poverty, we have developed an approach that recognises the contribution made by separate individuals in the household to the total household income, as well as the contribution made by other income sources such as pensions and benefits.

The procedure is as follows. Poor households are defined (as above) as those households with incomes below 60 per cent of median equivalised disposable household income, before housing costs. We then calculate whether the various sources of income are sufficient to take the household as a whole out of household poverty. The analysis starts by looking at whether a person's own market income takes the household above the poverty line; if not, partner's income is added on, then non-means-tested benefits are added on, and then successive types of income are added from a total of seven categories,[6] examining whether the household has crossed the poverty line by means of:

1   that individual's own market income

2   the addition of the market income of their partner

3   the addition of non-means-tested social security benefits

4   the addition of tax credits

5   the addition of means-tested social security benefits

6   the addition of the market incomes of other household members

7   the addition of other household income.

Some households are, of course, still in poverty after the final step.

The order in which income sources are added thus moves through own market income to the market income of partners and then to the various state transfers before including market income from others living in the household, and finally including any household income that cannot be readily attributed to individuals. This sequence is designed to reflect what we know – which is still quite limited – about how people perceive and value different sources of income and about the ways in which people living together pool their incomes. As regards income sources, various studies have shown that most people prefer to increase their incomes by additional work – second jobs or second earners – rather than by receipt of tax credits or benefits (McLaughlin et al., 1989; Jordan et al., 1992; Kempson, 1996; Kempson et al., 1996; Goode et al., 1998). Therefore, the earnings (and other market income) of self and a partner are placed first in the list. These studies also suggest that non-means-tested benefits are generally preferred to means-tested support, and this is also reflected in the ordering in the list. One of the government's main arguments for replacing family credit with a tax credit was that tax credits are less stigmatising and more acceptable than benefits (HM Treasury, 1998) and there is some evidence that families preferred the working families tax credit to family credit (McKay, 2002), although this may be more to do with the higher amounts that any intrinsic preference. Nevertheless we have placed tax credits above other means-tested benefits in our sequence.

The income of other household members, apart from a partner, is placed below benefits and tax credits in this list (unlike in Table 13 above). This is because, at this point in analysing the relationship between individual earnings and other sources of income, we are making a shift from 'family' or 'tax unit' income (i.e. the income of a single person, a lone-parent family, or a couple with or without dependent children) to total household income. In doing so we are, of necessity, making an assumption that there is income sharing within the whole household and not just within the family unit. We know that not all partners share all their income and that household financial allocation and management systems reflect differences in characteristics and circumstances, including income, employment status, age, and life-course position (Vogler and Pahl, 1993; Goode et al., 1998; Rake and Jayatilaka, 2002). But there is very little information available about income sharing within larger households. Placing the income of these others after the income of partners is intended to recognise the likelihood that such income may be even less likely than partner's income to be shared by all household members. Finally, all other income is added to the total. One component of this 'other income' is any regular allowance being received from outside the household, which includes maintenance payments. Arguably this might be preferred to income from state benefits, but it is not shown higher up the list of income sources because the data provide only a household total for this source of income and hence it cannot be allocated to any particular individual.

As shown above (in Table 11), about 5 per cent of all employees and about 14 per cent of low-paid employees are living in household poverty. Table 15 shows how employed people in non-poor households avoid household poverty. Among all employees, just over half – 53 per cent – have a market income that is high enough by itself to take the whole household out of poverty. For our sample (which excludes those who are primarily self-employed), this is almost entirely due to earnings rather than self-employment or investment income. Another 21 per cent have a partner with a market income which, when added to their own, takes the household out of poverty. This means that three-quarters of all employees avoid poverty by their own market income alone or in combination with their partner's market income. Benefits and tax credits play a relatively minor role in taking these households out of poverty, less so than income from other household members.

The situation looks quite different for the low-paid employees. Only 8 per cent of low-paid employees are able to take their households out of poverty by means of their market incomes alone (again it is earnings which are most important). Partner's income takes another 32 per cent across the poverty line. Benefits and tax credits take another 13 per cent above the poverty line, and 30 per cent avoid household poverty through the incomes of others in the household.

About 21 per cent of the low-paid employees are working less than 16 hours per week and it might be expected that these employees would be less able than others to avoid household poverty, in that they are both low-paid and work short hours.

Table 15   Avoiding poverty: all employees and low-paid employees, 2000/1

	All employees (%)	All low-paid employees (%)	Low-paid employees working 16 hours plus (%)
Own market income	53	8	9
Partner's market income	21	32	33
Non-means-tested benefits	5	8	8
Tax credits	1	2	3
Means-tested benefits	1	3	3
Others' income	13	30	29
Other household income	1	2	2
Remaining in poverty	5	14	14
Total	100	100	100
Unweighted base	(5,673)	(1,274)	(999)

However, as the final column of Table 15 shows, excluding these employees with short hours makes very little difference to the overall pattern of results.

Table 16 shows that hourly low-paid men and women avoid household poverty in rather different ways. The low-paid men are much more likely than the low-paid women to avoid poverty by means of their own market incomes (13 per cent compared with 4 per cent) and less likely to do so because of the addition of a partner's market income (11 per cent compared with 45 per cent). Benefits and tax credits play about the same role for low-paid men and women, but the men are more likely to avoid poverty by means of the incomes of other household members than are the women (42 per cent compared with 23 per cent).

These differences between men and women reflect different household circumstances. As we saw earlier, hourly low-paid men are more likely to be young and single, and often living with their parents. Figure 2 shows how low-paid men in different types of family avoid poverty. Breakdowns by gender and family type result in rather small sample sizes (shown in brackets on the graph), so these results should be interpreted with some caution. There are insufficient numbers of lone fathers for separate analysis.

As Figure 2 shows, low-paid single men rarely avoid poverty by means of their own market incomes but many do avoid household poverty because they live with other adults, typically, as we have seen, their parents. About 62 per cent avoid household poverty in this way. Men without children are the most likely to be able to avoid household poverty by means of their own wages alone (31 per cent), probably because they are working long weekly hours. Partner's market income takes another 40 per cent out of poverty. The two-earner combination is thus very important for these couples.

Table 16 Avoiding poverty: hourly low-paid employees by gender, 2000/1

	Men (%)	Women (%)
Own market income	13	4
Partner's market income	11	45
Non-means-tested benefits	8	9
Tax credits	2	3
Means-tested benefits	4	2
Others' income	42	23
Other household income	3	2
Remaining in poverty	17	13
Total	100	100

Figure 2   **Avoiding poverty: hourly low-paid men by family type, 2000/1**

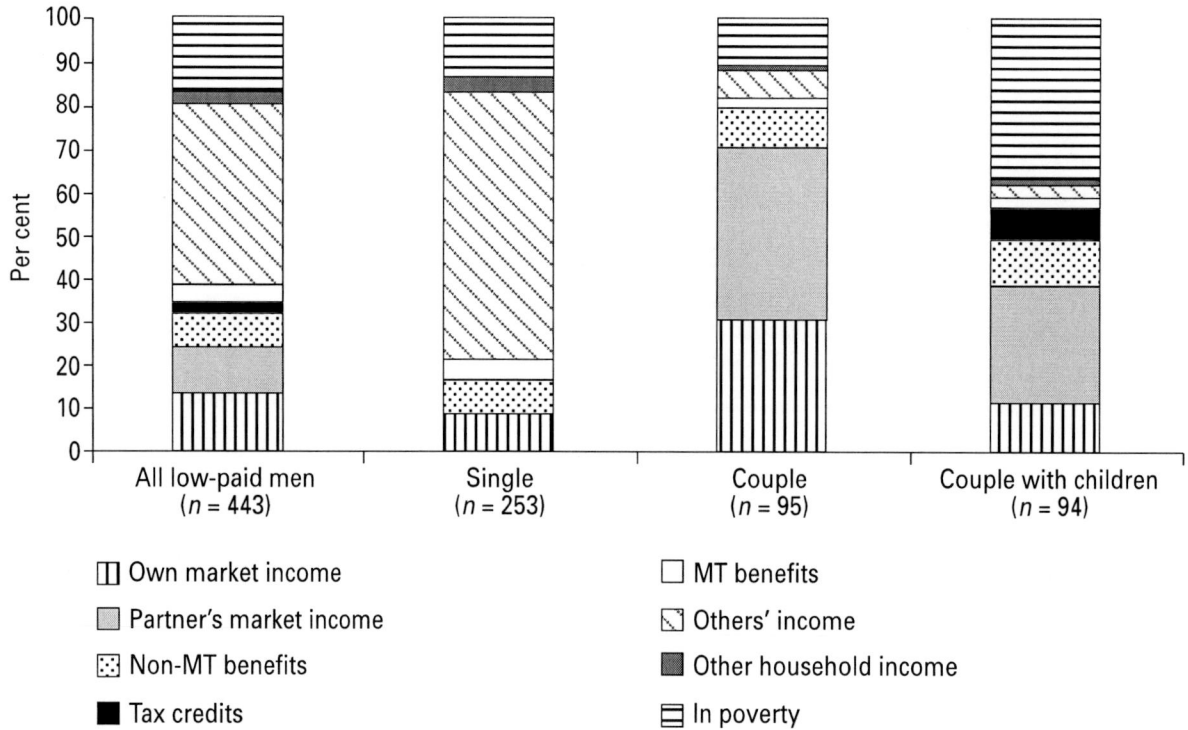

Legend:
- ⊞ Own market income
- ▨ Partner's market income
- ⊡ Non-MT benefits
- ■ Tax credits
- ☐ MT benefits
- ◺ Others' income
- ▦ Other household income
- ⊟ In poverty

The pattern is, however, quite different for men living in couples with dependent children. These men are not often able to take the household out of poverty by means of their own market incomes alone (11 per cent). Partner's market income takes another 27 per cent out of poverty and benefits and tax credits play an important role for these families, as might be expected (as those without children were not eligible for tax credits at that time). About 21 per cent of these families avoid poverty by means of tax credits and benefits. Nevertheless the low-paid men living in couples with children are the most likely to stay poor, with 37 per cent living in household poverty.

Figure 3 repeats this analysis for low-paid women. For single women without children, as for single men, the income of other household members plays an important role in helping the household avoid poverty. Nearly two in three (59 per cent) low-paid single women avoid poverty in this way. For low-paid women employees who are living in a couple without children, it is most commonly the market income (usually earnings) of their partner that help them to avoid poverty (71 per cent), and this group is the least likely to be in poverty (9 per cent). Those living in couples with children are also most likely to avoid household poverty by means of partner's market income (72 per cent), with a further 10 per cent avoiding poverty because of benefits or tax credits.

Figure 3   **Avoiding poverty: hourly low-paid women by family type, 2000/1**

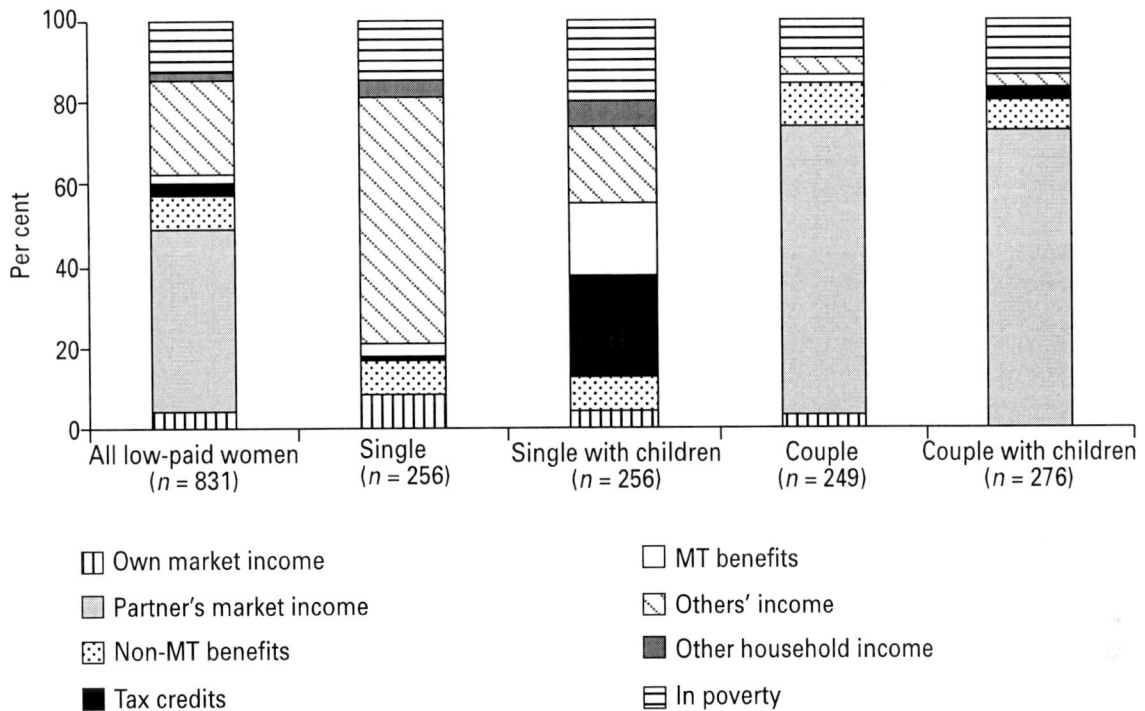

For low-paid lone mothers, benefits and tax credits are very important, taking about 51 per cent out of poverty, including 9 per cent by non-means-tested benefits, 25 per cent by tax credits and 17 per cent by means-tested benefits. Another 19 per cent of lone mothers avoid poverty because of the contribution of other household members, and a further 6 per cent as a result of other household income (which in this case is probably maintenance payments from an ex-partner). Nevertheless about 20 per cent of low-paid lone mothers remain in poverty.

The importance of tax credits for eligible lone mothers is shown even more clearly if we exclude those who were not eligible for the working families tax credit because they work for under 16 hours per week – about a third of our sample of low-paid lone mothers.[7] Over half (57 per cent) of the lone mothers working 16-plus hours per week avoid poverty by means of benefits and tax credits – 12 per cent by non-means-tested benefits, 40 per cent by tax credits and 5 per cent by means-tested benefits (although some of the sample sizes are small here). Another 20 per cent avoid poverty because of others' income. Other sources of household income, most likely child support payments, assist a further 9 per cent. This leaves just 8 per cent of these low-paid lone mothers working 16 hours plus in household poverty. Tax credits do not have this sort of impact for any other group.

Figure 4 focuses just on couples and compares those with one or two earners (where 'earner' refers to our definition of employee and hence excludes the self-employed). When a low-paid person is the sole earner the household has a very high risk of poverty, whether the employee is a woman (31 per cent in poverty) or a man (50 per cent in poverty). For the low-paid women, partner's market income (not wages but self-employment or unearned income) takes about 37 per cent of these households out of poverty. This clearly shows that, even for our sample of employees, sources of market income other than earnings can play an important role in households with low-paid employees. Obviously the impact of these sources would probably be even more significant if we were looking at a more broadly defined sample of income earners than just employees and their households. The low-paid sole-earner men are more likely than their female counterparts to take the household out of poverty by means of just their own market income. But their partners rarely have any non-wage market income, unlike the men partners of low-paid women. For the two-earner couples, it is the fact of having two sources of earnings that is crucial in keeping poverty rates down. For both low-paid men and women in two-earner couples, their partner's market income is more important in avoiding household poverty than their own, this being particularly true for the women.

Figure 4   Avoiding poverty: hourly low-paid employees in couples by number of earners, 2000/1

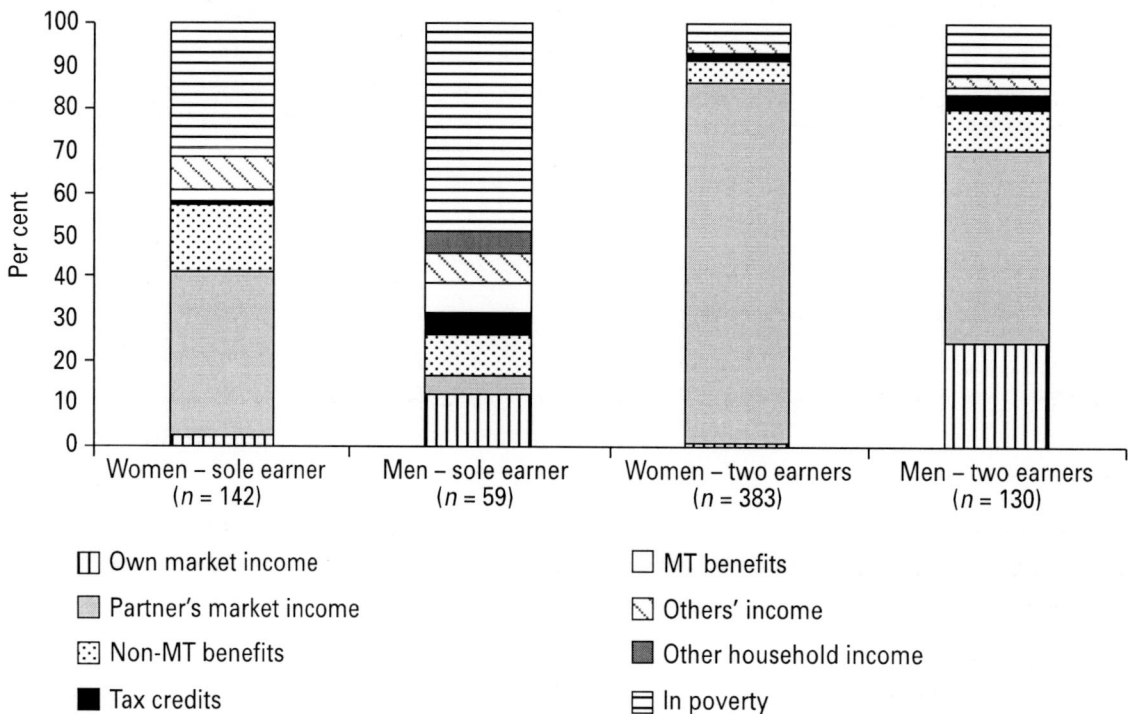

Comparisons of 2000/1 with 1994/5

Table 17 compares the avoidance of poverty among low-paid employees in 1994/5 and 2000/1. As discussed above, our estimates show that the proportion of low-paid people living in household poverty rose slightly over this time period, from 11 per cent to 14 per cent. But in general the picture as regards poverty avoidance looks very similar in both years. There is no change in the proportion who avoid household poverty by means of their own market incomes, 8 per cent in both years. Partner's income took about 37 per cent out of household poverty in 1994/5 and 32 per cent in 2000/1. It is perhaps surprising that the impact of partner's income has fallen over this period and this may reflect further concentration of labour market disadvantage within families. Benefits and tax credits (or their equivalent in 1994/5) enabled about 14 per cent to avoid poverty in both years.

However, as we discussed earlier, trends in the overlap between low pay and poverty were different for different types of family (see Table 12). The overlap between low pay and household poverty for low-paid employees increased between 1994/5 and 2000/1 for single men and for men in couples without children. Looking specifically at these groups gives some indication of what happened to their household incomes. Table 18 shows that among low-paid single men the main difference is that the importance of others' income has declined. For low-paid men in couples without children, own market income is much less effective in avoiding household poverty, although partner's income increased in importance.

Table 19 presents a similar analysis for low-paid lone mothers, the group for whom there was the most dramatic decline in poverty rates between 1994/5 and 2000/1, particularly when we look only at those working 16 hours or more. What is most striking in the analysis of income sources and income providers underlying this change is the marked increase in the contribution of market income from other

Table 17 Avoiding poverty: low-paid employees, 1994/5 and 2000/1

	1994/5 (%)	2000/1 (%)
Own market income	8	8
Partner's market income	37	32
Non-means-tested benefits	9	8
Tax credits[a]	2	2
Means-tested benefits	4	3
Others' income	27	30
Other sources of income	2	2
Remaining in poverty	11	14
Total	100	100

a   For 1994/5, 'tax credits' refers to the benefits in 1994/5 which were subsequently replaced by tax credits, i.e. Family Credit and Disability Working Allowance.

Table 18 Avoiding poverty: low-paid men by selected family type, 1994/5 and 2000/1

	Single men (%)		Men in couples, no children (%)	
	1994/5	2000/1	1994/5	2000/1
Own market income	8	9	49	31
Partner's market income	0	0	31	40
Non-means-tested benefits	9	7	9	9
Tax credits[a]	*	0	0	0
Means-tested benefits	4	5	1	3
Others' income	69	62	5	6
Other sources of income	4	3	1	1
Remaining in poverty	5	14	3	11
Unweighted base	(213)	(253)	(74)	(95)

a   For 1994/5, 'tax credits' refers to the benefits in 1994/5 which were subsequently replaced by tax credits i.e. Family Credit and Disability Working Allowance.

Note: * is used for numbers below 0.5.

adults. In 1994/5 about 8 per cent were taken over the poverty line by the income of others in the household; by 2000/1 this had more than doubled to 19 per cent. As we saw in Table 14 these other adults are mainly non-dependent children, and this change over time may reflect the older age profile of lone mothers over this period, so that more are likely to have their young adult children living at home. It may also reflect the fact that it has become increasingly difficult for these young adults to set up their own households.

The other interesting result from Table 19 is the offsetting effects on poverty rates of lone parents' own market income, on the one hand, and tax credits and benefits, on the other. Benefits and tax credits have increased in importance since the mid-1990s, taking 51 per cent out of poverty by 2000/1 compared with 45 per cent in 1994/5. Looking just at those working for 16 hours plus (the group eligible for tax credits), the increase is even greater, from 48 per cent to 57 per cent. The figures suggest that as tax credits have been made more generous they have become more effective than their predecessor in-work benefits (labelled in the 1994/5 columns as 'tax credits' for ease of comparison) and this gain has not been completely offset by corresponding reductions in the impact of means-tested benefits (from 6 to 5 per cent), so that there has been an overall increase in effectiveness of these combined transfers as anti-poverty measures. However, the increased generosity of tax credits does not appear to have had the desired knock-on effect on the ability of lone parents to help themselves, with in fact fewer low-paid lone parents avoiding poverty on the basis of their own market income in 2000/1, compared with 1994/5.

Table 19 Avoiding poverty: low-paid women by selected family type, 1994/5 and 2000/1

	Lone mothers (%)		Lone mothers working 16 hours plus (%)	
	1994/5	2000/1	1994/5	2000/1
Own market income	7	4	9	6
Partner's market income	0	0	0	0
Non-means-tested benefits	5	9	9	12
Tax credits[a]	19	25	33	40
Means-tested benefits	21	17	6	5
Others' income	8	19	13	20
Other sources of income	13	6	9	9
Remaining in poverty	28	20	22	8
Unweighted base	(77)	(50)	(46)	(33)

a   For 1994/5, 'tax credits' refers to the benefits in 1994/5 which were subsequently replaced by tax credits i.e. Family Credit and Disability Working Allowance.

When we look at other low-paid workers with children, in Table 20, we see that both men and women in couples with children saw no real change in their risk of poverty between 1994/5 and 2000/1. This is in contrast to the improvement in poverty rates for lone mothers and the worsening of poverty for men and women without children (whether single or in a couple). When we examine the importance of different income sources for avoiding poverty, the results for both men and women in couples with children show that men's market income has become less effective in avoiding poverty for these households but this has been compensated for by a rise in the positive impact of tax credits and benefits.

Table 20 Avoiding poverty: low-paid men and women in couples with children, 1994/5 and 2000/1

	Men in couples with children (%)		Women in couples, with children (%)	
	1994/5	2000/1	1994/5	2000/1
Own market income	15	11	*	*
Partner's market income	27	27	74	72
Non-means-tested benefits	7	11	3	7
Tax credits[a]	5	7	1	3
Means-tested benefits	6	3	3	0
Others' income	3	2	4	4
Other sources of income	0	2	1	0
Remaining in poverty	37	37	14	13
Unweighted base	(67)	(94)	(320)	(276)

a   For 1994/5, 'tax credits' refers to the benefits in 1994/5 which were subsequently replaced by tax credits i.e. Family Credit and Disabled Working Allowance.

Note: * is used for numbers below 0.5.

Summary

Paid work does substantially reduce the risk of household poverty. One-fifth of all individuals live in poor households compared with about 5 per cent of employees. But hourly low-paid people have a much higher risk of living in household poverty than those who are not low-paid – 14 per cent compared with 2 per cent. Low-paid men are more likely to be living in poor households than low-paid women.

The overlap between hourly low pay and household poverty has increased slightly since the mid-1990s, continuing a trend over time. In the 1970s and 1980s the overlap between low pay and poverty was only around 3 to 4 per cent of low-paid employees, compared with 14 per cent in 2000/1.

Among low-paid men it is those with children who are most likely to be in household poverty, with 37 per cent poor. This has not changed since the mid-1990s, but for other low-paid men the situation has got worse. For example, in 1994/5 about 5 per cent of single low-paid men were living in household poverty. By 2000/1 this had risen almost threefold to 14 per cent. Single low-paid women also experienced an increase in their risk of household poverty. But for low-paid lone mothers there was a fall in the proportion of household poverty, from 28 per cent to 20 per cent.

For the majority of low-paid people who do not live in household poverty, we have identified which sources of income coming into the household are taking the household out of poverty. Rarely do low-paid people avoid household poverty by their own wages alone, although men can do this more often than women, probably by working long weekly hours. Living with other people – partners and, just as importantly, other adults – who have earnings or other market income is very important in helping those with low hourly wages to reach adequate weekly incomes. The fall in poverty rates for low-paid lone mothers since the mid-1990s appears to be linked to the greater impact of income from other adults in the household, most often their grown-up children.

Being a sole earner in a couple substantially increases the poverty risk. Low-paid single-earner couples have a very high poverty risk, especially for sole-earner men. Sole-earner women often have partners with some other market income, or income from pensions, but the men single earners do not. Tax credits and benefits are important for families with children, especially lone mothers.

Placing low-paid people in the context of their wider families and households thus shows that the most successful way to avoid living in household poverty if you are low-paid is through the people with whom you live, provided of course that those people are indeed pooling their incomes with you. Transfers through the tax and benefit system also help those with children, but only for low-paid lone mothers are these transfers the dominant means of avoiding poverty.

4 Summary, discussion and policy issues

This study of low pay and poverty has tackled three main topics: the extent of low pay among people in different family types; the overlap between individual low pay and household poverty; and the access to other income sources that enable some low-paid people to avoid poverty. There are few other studies which have considered this last issue, but examining the household incomes of low-paid workers who are not in poor households enables us to start to disentangle the complex relationships between individual and household circumstances, and the role of government policy in this.

The analysis shows that, for households, having income from paid work is indeed the most successful way to avoid poverty. But for individual workers, avoiding poverty depends not just on one's own wages, but also on other circumstances. About a quarter of all employees are in low-paid jobs and these workers' own earnings are rarely high enough to keep them out of poverty, unless they work very long hours each week. If they are the sole earners for their families, then the risk of living in household poverty is high. If they live with others, and those others also have jobs or other sources of market income, then the risk of poverty is much reduced. In-work benefits and tax credits can play a similar role for some families – particularly lone parents – but not to the same extent as market income. Thus more accurate than the slogan 'work is the best route out of poverty' is the following statement: having a job *and* living with other people with jobs is the most likely way of avoiding poverty.

In this final chapter, we start by summarising the key findings from this analysis and then discuss the policy issues and implications.

Low pay and household status

About 5.4 million people were low-paid in 2000/1 – that is, their hourly earnings were below two-thirds of the median for all employees. This was one in four of all employees, with women facing a higher risk of being low-paid (30 per cent) than men (18 per cent), so that women make up three-fifths of all low-paid employees. Just over half of low-paid women work part-time but most low-paid men work full-time. The risk of low pay has been falling for women and rising for men, and whereas women in 2000/1 were 1.7 times as likely to be low-paid as men, in 1968 they were six times as likely. In absolute terms, the number of low-paid men has about doubled in the past 30 or so years, while the number of low-paid women has hardly changed.

The groups most at risk of hourly low pay are young and single people, but the majority of low-paid people do not fit these categories: half are aged between 22 and 49, half are in couples, and a third have children. Over half (53 per cent) of low-paid people live in households with other adults (apart from their partner) compared with one-third (34 per cent) of employees in general. If they are single this usually means their parents and sometimes their siblings. About seven in ten single low-paid men live in such households. One-third of low-paid lone parents live with others, usually their adult children.

Thus many low-paid single people and lone parents potentially have other working people in the household. People living in couples are less likely to live with others who may bring income into the household, but this can be compensated by the fact that their partner may have earnings (or other income). However, someone in a couple who is low-paid is less likely than most employees in couples to have a working partner. Even where they do work, partners of low-paid men and women are more likely than average to be low-paid themselves. Hourly low-paid people tend to work shorter hours than employees in general, compounding low hourly pay into low weekly earnings. On the other hand, some hourly low-paid men work very long hours and so avoid weekly low pay.

Low pay and household poverty

Most employees are not living in poor households and this is also true for low-paid employees. But low-paid employees are almost three times as likely as all employees to be living in household poverty (14 per cent compared with 5 per cent in 2000/1). The overlap between low pay and poverty was very low in the 1960s and 1970s, but as the numbers of low-paid people with dependants has increased so has the overlap between low pay and poverty, from around 3 to 4 per cent in the late 1960s to around 14 per cent in 2000/1. Since the mid-1990s, low-paid people without children have become more likely to be poor, but there has been a significant drop in the risk of poverty for lone parents on low pay: from 28 per cent to 20 per cent. Low-paid men in couples with children remain at the greatest risk, along with their families: almost four in ten are in poor households.

How low-paid people avoid poverty

We examined how households avoid poverty by looking first at whether a low-paid person's wages are sufficient to do this alone, and then successively adding in other income sources to see which, if any, takes the household over the poverty line.

Overall only 8 per cent of low-paid people are able to take their household out of poverty by means of their own wages alone, compared with 53 per cent of all employees. This is a substantial difference and means that low-paid people must rely on other sources of income coming into the household if they are to avoid poverty. Compared with other employees, fewer low-paid people have partners with income, but more live in households with income from benefits, tax credits and other adults.

There are clear differences by family type in respect of both whether someone who is low-paid can avoid poverty and, if so, how they do this:

• Of single low-paid people, about six out of seven were able to avoid poverty. It is the market income of others in their household, typically parents, that most often makes the difference.

• Of couples, about nine in ten of those without children avoided poverty, as did eight in ten of those with children, but this was the case for fewer men (63 per cent) than women (87 per cent). It is the joint earnings of the two partners that are crucial. Couples with just one low-paid earner are at a very high risk of poverty and although benefits and tax credits do help couples with children, in general these transfers are not nearly as effective as having a second earner in the family.

• Low-paid lone mothers are as likely to avoid poverty as low-paid two-parent families (80 per cent). For these lone-parent families, more than any others, benefits and tax credits play a significant role. In particular, over half (57 per cent) of low-paid lone mothers working 16 or more hours per week avoid poverty by receipt of benefits and tax credits. Tax credits take about 40 per cent of them over the poverty line. Living with others – usually adult children – is also often important.

There are also some differences by family type in respect of how things have changed since the mid-1990s:

• The risk of living in a poor household had increased almost threefold for low-paid single men and low-paid men in couples with no dependent children by 2000/1. The single men are less likely to avoid poverty by the income of others in their households. The men in couples with no dependent children have become less likely to be able to avoid poverty by their own earnings and, although their partners' incomes are playing a larger role, this has not fully compensated. These childless people have not, until very recently, been eligible for much tax or benefit support although they have now been brought within the tax credit net (see further discussion below).

- The risk of living in a poor household has fallen for low-paid lone mothers, and especially for low-paid lone mothers working 16 hours or more per week. For all lone mothers, the main change underlying this improvement has been the increased importance of others' market income. This has also helped lone mothers working 16 hours or more, but for them tax credits and benefits have played a more significant role in their reduced risk of poverty. However, even for the lone mothers entitled to claim tax credits their own wages are actually less likely to take them out of poverty.

- For low-paid workers, both men and women, who live in couples and have dependent children, the risk of poverty hardly changed between 1994/5 and 2000/1. Our results suggest that men's earnings have become less able to keep their households out of poverty but this has been offset by a rise in the contribution of tax credits and benefits.

Figure 5 summarises the overall picture in 2000/1, showing the numbers of people who are low-paid by family type, and the numbers who are low-paid and also living in household poverty. This shows, for example, that whereas nearly five times as many young single people as fathers are low-paid, similar numbers of people in these two groups are in poverty.

Figure 5   Low pay and household poverty in 2000/1: number by family type

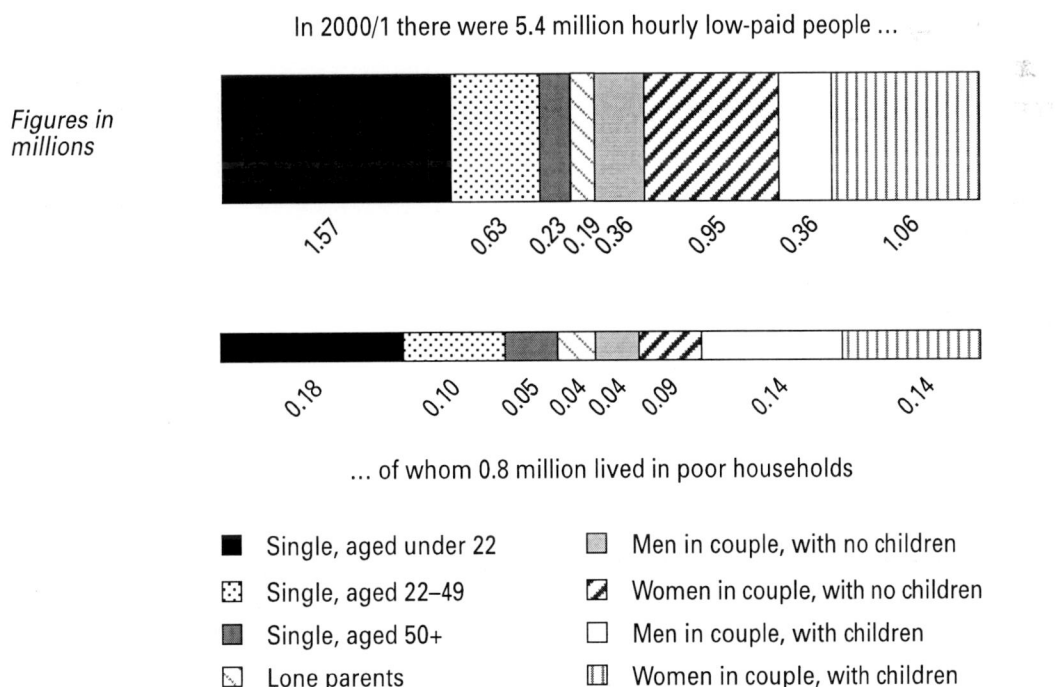

In 2000/1 there were 5.4 million hourly low-paid people ...

Figures in millions

1.57   0.63   0.23 0.19 0.36   0.95   0.36   1.06

0.18   0.10   0.05 0.04 0.04   0.09   0.14   0.14

... of whom 0.8 million lived in poor households

■ Single, aged under 22   ▨ Men in couple, with no children

▨ Single, aged 22–49   ▨ Women in couple, with no children

▨ Single, aged 50+   ☐ Men in couple, with children

▨ Lone parents   ▥ Women in couple, with children

Employment has been rising in recent years and the number of households with all adults in work rose from 10.5 million in 1996 to 11.8 million in 2002 (Gregg and Wadsworth, 2003). However, as we have seen, not all those who are in work can avoid poverty, and our analysis shows that whether or not low-paid people manage to avoid poverty depends both on their household circumstances and on whether they receive in-work benefits or tax credits to boost their incomes. Other studies use different methods but reach similar conclusions. For example, Jenkins and Rigg (2001, p. 4), in their analysis of the dynamics of poverty, emphasise 'the relative importance of the labour market in providing a route out of poverty for individuals of working age' and conclude that the current focus of promoting work is therefore the right approach but that for some groups additional measures – like tax credits and other in-work supports – are needed. They also show that having other working people in the household is an important factor in reducing the risk of becoming and staying poor: as they put it, 'how well off you are, and how your living standards change from one year to the next, depend on who you live with, what they do, and what happens to them' (p. 4).

Sutherland *et al.* (2003, p. 24) conclude that the fall in child poverty since 1997 has been achieved by two main routes. First 'unemployment fell and more households had someone in paid employment'. Second, 'policy on benefits and tax credits clearly disadvantaged some and helped others'. Children in unemployed or inactive families generally stayed poor, despite some increases in the level of child-related benefits for non-employed families. But working families were helped by the extension of in-work support and 'those more likely to gain were those with children, particularly low earners in employment, and this was a major factor in the reduction by some half a million in the number of children in poverty'.

Both wages and tax/benefit transfers are thus necessary for many low-paid workers to avoid poverty. This raises important questions about whether the balance between policies intended to increase pay and those intended to increase incomes in work is appropriate, and whether in-work transfers are adequate and effectively targeted. However, before going on to consider policy issues and implications, the next section discusses the various poverty avoidance strategies that we have identified and analysed.

Poverty avoidance strategies: reflections

In looking at the overlap between low pay and poverty we have outlined various strategies that people who are at high risk of poverty because of low pay could potentially adopt. The strategies we have considered are, very broadly speaking, working long hours, living with working partners, claiming benefits and tax credits, and living with other working people.

As we noted at the start, not all these strategies are available to all people in the same way. What determines the strategies people actually use will depend on a number of factors. First, it will depend on what options are available to them: for example, what market wage they can command, the availability of suitable jobs where they live and whether or not they qualify for (and claim) tax credits/benefits. Second, the strategies they adopt will reflect their preferences and constraints: for example, their life-course stage in relation to both employment (whether they are just starting out in the labour market or closer to retirement) and family formation (whether they have a partner and/or children); whether they have other ways they can meet their needs (for example, inherited income, self-employment, self-sufficiency); the costs associated with work (for example, travel cost, travel time, childcare costs); and other factors apart from income that affect their well-being (for example, spending time with their family). Furthermore, we are only looking at poverty at a single point in time yet individuals may face a trade-off between avoiding poverty today versus avoiding poverty in the future. Hence, they may decide to take a low-pay job or invest in their education even though it means their income falls below the poverty line, because this will improve their future income prospects.

The outcome, in terms of the strategies that we observe people using at any point in time, will vary according to these and other factors that influence their options and therefore their behaviour. Furthermore, individuals may use certain strategies without this being part of a conscious intention to avoid poverty – for example, people live with extended family because they want to and not because they want to share incomes. In analysing the data and in reflecting on policy implications, we have tried to avoid making value judgements about these strategies, not least because we do not have complete information about current circumstances or future plans. Our aim has been to identify which strategies at a particular point in time are most effective in avoiding financial poverty, with a focus on paid work, and how this varies for people living in different sorts of families and households.

Hence, while we have not considered the potential advantages and disadvantages of different strategies, other than their effect on avoiding household income poverty, these will affect individuals' decisions about the suitable strategies for them to adopt. For example:

• Living with others and sharing their income has the potential problem of what happens if individuals leave or the household splits up. This could lead to a very high poverty risk for some people in the household.

• There are costs in respect of time poverty if most people in the family or household are working, and especially if they work long hours.

- Claiming benefits/tax credits can create poverty traps so that it is difficult to increase income by working more or getting a better-paid job.

- Young people may sacrifice their independence if they continue living with their parents.

These sorts of issues highlight the point that governments must take political decisions about which strategies to support and promote and which to leave more to personal preference. For example, living with extended family is, our results suggest, an effective way for some low-paid people to avoid poverty, but promoting this as government policy may not be appropriate in the context of other government objectives for individuals to take more personal responsibility for themselves. The decisions that governments take to support one strategy rather than another will also have an impact on the relative effectiveness of the different strategies. Thus, for example, the current policy of promoting paid work as the main route out of poverty will, if effective, increase the relative attraction of this strategy compared with others. However, this focus on paid work has been criticised as reducing options for some people, and in particular as reducing the options for parents to provide full-time care for children or to combine paid work and care in different ways at different times (Bennett and Hirsch, 2001; Williams, 2004).

Reducing low pay, reducing poverty: policy implications

Our analysis referred to the period up to 2000/1. Since then there have been a number of policy developments:

- The national minimum wage has been regularly increased. By 2003, it was up to £4.50 per hour for the adult rate and £3.80 per hour for the youth/training rate. From October 2004, the adult rate will be £4.85 per hour and the youth rate will be £4.10. Young workers aged 16 to 17 will also be included with a national minimum wage rate of £3.00 per hour. It is estimated by the government that around 1.6 and 1.9 million people will benefit from this increase (HM Treasury, 2004).

- The child tax credit and the working tax credit were introduced from April 2003 to replace the working families tax credit and the disabled person's tax credit. Single people and childless couples are, for the first time, eligible for tax credits but only those who are working 30 hours or more per week. By January 2004, about 6.1 million people were receiving the child tax credit and/or the working tax credit, including 4.7 million people in work (Inland Revenue, 2004).

- The government has also continued to expand and develop the welfare-to-work measures, through the New Deal programmes and through various pilot schemes intended to support job search, to help people make the transition into work, and to help those who do find jobs to stay in work. Mandatory work-focused interviews have been introduced for more groups of claimants, including lone parents, partners of unemployed claimants, and some people claiming incapacity benefits.

These measures thus represent a continuation and strengthening of the 'make work pay' approach, combining, as before, provisions targeted on individuals and those targeted on families, but extending to more groups of workers.

In respect of policy implications, Hills (2001) provides a useful framework for analysing policies according to the type of outcome they are intended to influence. He distinguishes between four main types of intervention: *prevention* to reduce the risk of entering a negative situation; *protection* from the adverse consequences of being in that situation; *promotion* of exit or escape from that situation; and *propulsion* to help people move further away from the negative situation.

In relation to low pay, prevention arguably lies mainly with policies to develop human capital, to improve education and skills and so to increase productivity. These sorts of measures could also enable promotion of exit and propulsion away from disadvantage, reducing the risk of low pay in the future as well as the present. However, alongside human capital measures, low pay could also be prevented by a higher national minimum wage, by greater equality of wages between women and men, and between part-time and full-time workers. The Low Pay Commission (2004) recommends that the national minimum wage could be further increased without adverse consequences for employment, and various groups, including the Trades Union Congress, Church Action on Poverty and TELCO, have argued for a 'living wage' that is closer to our low pay threshold of two-thirds of the median.[1]

Means-tested support in work, by contrast, may act as a brake on promotion of exit from low pay and on propulsion away. Using means-tested support to boost low pay inevitably contributes to a 'poverty trap', when people in work have limited incentive to improve their earnings because of the consequent loss of benefits. The introduction of the second generation of tax credits has reduced the number of people with very high 'marginal deduction rates' (how much of each additional £ of gross earnings is lost through higher taxes and withdrawn tax credits or benefits) but increased the number of people with marginal deduction rates of between 60 and 70 per cent (HM Treasury, 2004). The provision within the tax credits scheme to ignore pay increases of up to £2,500 in the tax year in which they occur means that people do not have to face a reduction in tax credits as soon as they receive an increase in gross earnings. This should provide an important cushion, enabling people to increase their earnings without immediate penalty. In the longer term, however, subsidising wages for all low-paid workers may reduce the opportunities for propulsion out of low pay (Bennett and Hirsch, 2001). There is a risk that a 'Speenhamland' effect – whereby employers pay lower wages in the knowledge that these will be topped up by government transfers – will develop over time.

However, our main focus in this research has been on the extent to which the current approach provides *protection from poverty for low-paid workers*, and our results show that there is indeed a problem to be addressed here. Low-paid people do have a high risk of poverty and the fact that many of them avoid it by living with others does not mean that policy can neglect their needs. Not everyone has the opportunity to share households with other earners, and for those who do, living with others may sometimes be an unwelcome consequence of poverty resulting from low pay, rather than a way of living that they have chosen freely. As discussed above, there are various constraints on the strategies that people can use to avoid poverty.

Our analysis suggests that it would be helpful to consider the needs of different groups of low-paid people separately. For low-paid *single people*, it is family support rather than the tax/benefit system that is currently helping most of them to avoid poverty. Of course, this is not a valid conclusion if these households are not pooling incomes and sharing resources, but it is likely that many parents are in effect subsidising their adult children who are working in low-paid jobs. Opportunities for financial independence, in the sense of having an adequate income to support oneself, are thus limited for these low-paid single people. HM Treasury (2004) estimates that the 'weekly minimum guarantee' for a single person, aged 25 or over, working 35 hours per week is about £164 per week in 2004, an increase from £113 in 1999. This is above the poverty line for a single person but this 'minimum guarantee' does not apply to younger single people, since under-22 year olds do not get the adult rate of the national minimum wage and under-25 year olds are not eligible for working tax credit. Nor does it apply to people without children working under 30 hours, who have no entitlement to working tax credit.

One option would be to continue to rely on families to provide additional support and adequate living standards for low-paid single people. This is how most low-paid young people avoid poverty, it is the least costly option for the government, and it seems to have worked well in the past. However, our analysis suggests that low pay is increasingly extending beyond the first years of working life. Parents may find it increasingly difficult to support adult children over long periods of time and it could be argued that it is not appropriate for young adults to be financially dependent in this way. Young single workers rarely have other sources of individual (as opposed to household) income, so the national minimum wage is very important to them. The Low Pay Commission (2004) recommends that the adult rate should include 21 year olds (rather than those aged 22 and over), while the introduction of a national minimum wage for 16 to 17 year olds (announced in the 2004 Budget) will help those very young workers. We have yet to see the impact of extending tax credits to single people, but so far the numbers registered for the credit are quite low, about 180,000 in total, and about 50,000 of these have zero awards.[2] However, the childless recipients tend to be older, rather than younger, workers with just 2 per cent aged under 24 and 56 per cent aged between 40 and 59 (Inland Revenue, 2004). Bringing young people into both the adult national minimum wage and the tax credit system at the age of 21 would align these two types of support and extend the minimum income guarantee to a wider group of young workers.

Low-paid *lone parents,* like single workers without children, can rarely avoid poverty by means of just their wages alone. But for these families there is some evidence that the current approach has been relatively successful in increasing employment, in making work pay and in reducing the risk of poverty in work. As we have shown, living with other people, typically adult children, is also an important factor in helping low-paid lone parents to avoid poverty. Various studies have shown a positive impact of tax credits on employment rates for lone parents (Brewer *et al.*, 2003; Gregg and Harkness, 2003; Francesconi and van der Klaauw, 2004), and our analysis shows that the introduction of tax credits has meant less poverty for working lone-parent families if they work 16 hours or more. Just over half of all lone parents are employed, so increasing employment rates is a priority, especially in the context of the target of 70 per cent employment by 2010. About a quarter of employed lone parents are low-paid, but for those working at least 16 hours per week the combination of wages, child benefit, tax credits, other means-tested benefits and child support does provide most lone parents with an income above the poverty line in work. Receipt of the new tax credits is high among lone parents. In January 2004 there were about a million working lone parents receiving tax credits, about 834,000 receiving both working tax credit and child tax credit and about 193,000 receiving just the child tax credit (Inland Revenue, 2004).

However, for working lone parents there is quite a complex income package required to avoid in-work poverty and this can be difficult to set up, making the transition into work problematic. Increasing the level of the child tax credit (rather than the working tax credit) would help to smooth the transition into work and be in line with the Work and Pensions Select Committee (2001) view that the maximum award of child tax credit should reflect the actual costs of children. In addition the costs of working – especially childcare and travel – can significantly reduce the financial returns from work. Increasing the contribution to childcare costs would help lone parents to meet these costs and enable them to have a greater choice of the type of provision. This could be done through increasing the child tax credit itself, or by extending the coverage and level of the childcare tax credit, or through subsidies to childcare suppliers (IFS (2003) models various options for childcare costs).

For low-paid people living in *couples*, the best way to avoid poverty is employment for both. This is especially effective for low-paid women, whose partners when employed tend not to be low-paid. But low-paid men often have either non-employed partners or partners who are also low-paid. For these couples, tax credits can provide a valuable addition to low wages. Like single people, childless couples have just been brought into eligibility for working tax credit, as long as the claimant is employed for over 30 hours per week. However, the number of claimants is low, just 94,000 (of whom 41,000 have zero awards). Just under half of childless couples receiving working tax credit are couples with a male sole earner, 23 per cent have a female sole earner and 30 per cent are two-earner couples. Couples with dependent children can claim working tax credit if one (or both) work for 16 or more hours per week. In January 2004 there were about 755,000 couples with children receiving both working tax credit and child tax credit, and another 2.5 million receiving child tax credit only. Of those receiving the working tax credit, 62 per cent were male sole earners, 14 per cent were female sole earners and 24 per cent were dual-earner families (Inland Revenue, 2004). Take-up figures are not yet available for the new tax credits, but couples had lower take-up rates than lone parents for working families tax credit, and for family credit before that (McKay, 2002), so there is likely to be some non-take-up reducing the anti-poverty impact. A commitment to ensuring that the take-up of tax credits is at least at the same level as that of lone parents would be a worthwhile goal.

Raising the level of tax credit support for couples would be one way to increase their in-work incomes. Hillman (2004), for example, argues that the current system penalises couples relative to lone parents and makes it more difficult to achieve the anti-poverty goals. This is because the basic rates of tax credits are the same for couples and for lone parents[3] and thus 'do not recognise the extra costs of a second adult being present' (p. 70). This means that the tax credits are out of step with the way in which Households Below Average Income poverty figures are calculated (where couples are weighted as having higher needs than lone parents). Thus couples receiving tax credits may be below the poverty line just because the two systems are, in effect, using different equivalence scales.[4] This would suggest that the couple rate should be higher than the rate for lone parents. On the other hand, it could be argued that the rates reflect a family premium and so the appropriate dividing line is between those with and those without children and not between couples and lone parents.

Another issue for couples concerns the position of second earners. Tax credits make work pay by boosting family income when wages are low. But the family-based means test used to determine eligibility for tax credits creates a potential disincentive for second earners. If the family is a one-earner couple and the other partner starts work, then tax credits will be reduced accordingly, after the £2,500 disregard is applied. If the family incurs childcare costs because both are working, only part of these will be met, which may be a further disincentive for the second earner. Our results (and other research) highlight the importance of having two earners in the family as the most effective way to avoid poverty. So a system that potentially discourages second earners seems a perverse way to try and increase family income. However, Brewer *et al.* (2003) find only a small effect of the working tax credit on the employment of mothers in couples. They estimate that the working families tax credit increased the employment of fathers in couples by 0.8 percentage points and reduced the employment of mothers in couples by 0.2 percentage points. Evidence from the operation of family credit also suggests that, in practice, couples respond more to labour market opportunities than they do to incentives or disincentives created by the tax and benefit system (Bryson and Marsh, 1996). On the other hand, however, women seem to be more responsive to these financial incentives and disincentives than do men.

The family basis of this means test also seems contradictory in the context of other moves towards greater individualisation in the benefit system, and in relation to the focus on the importance of individual rights and responsibilities, particularly in respect of labour market participation issues. For example, joint claims are now required for childless people claiming jobseeker's allowance, there are compulsory work-focused interviews for partners of recipients of jobseeker's allowance and incapacity benefits, and the New Deal for Partners offers job search advice and assistance on a voluntary basis. The partners of tax credit recipients are also eligible for New Deal support, and the 2004 Budget report announced a pilot scheme to extend the 'work search premium' of £20 per week to non-workers in families receiving working tax credit (HM Treasury, 2004).

Arguably the issues are different for child tax credit and working tax credit. Child tax credit is intended as a contribution to the support of children, and thus a family-based means test, which takes account of the incomes of both parents, is the most appropriate way to do this (Millar, 2004). Working tax credit, however, is a supplement to individual wages and so might more appropriately be assessed on individual earnings rather than family income. This might, however, increase the risk of a further downward shift on wages. A less radical alternative would be a second-earner disregard, in addition to the general £2,500 disregard, so that couples would not face a 100 per cent withdrawal rate on second earnings.

One of the main arguments for introducing the two tax credits (working tax credit and the child tax credit) to replace the working families tax credit was to match policy instruments with policy goals. 'Using one system to achieve two objectives – in the case of Working Families Tax Credit, better work incentives and increased family support – can give rise to tensions' (HM Treasury, 2000, p. 12). But the stated goal of the working tax credit – to make work pay – can mean a number of different things and a number of policy aims are still rolled up in this one transfer. For example, helping people to make the transition into work might be better served by a flat-rate time-limited payment (like the now abolished 50-plus credit or the lone parent in-work credit which will be available from October 2004 in 12 pilot areas, providing a payment of £40 per week for the first 12 months of employment). Helping families to meet needs during a period when one parent is providing full-time care for children might be better served by a system of paid parental leave, with the right of return to work protected. Such measures would make the in-work financial system more complex and there is a trade-off to be made between a single system trying to cover lots of needs at the same time and a more differentiated system treating each of these differently. But as in-work supplementation comes to occupy a more central place in policy it will be increasingly important to address directly these questions of goals and targeting.

Notes

Chapter 1

1   More accurately, low-income families with at least one person in paid work.

Chapter 2

1   Since 2001/2, the Family Expenditure Survey has been combined with the National Food Survey, and is now called the Expenditure and Food Survey.

2   For more details see www.esds.ac.uk/government/fes

3   There are two main rates, the adult rate for those aged 22 and above, the youth and development rate for those aged between 18 and 21, and those undertaking accredited training in the first six months of a new job. For a chronology of policy developments in relation to the national minimum wage, see http://www.dti.gov.uk/er/nmw/nmwhist.htm

4   Table A1 presents comparable results to Table 3, using two alternative definitions of hourly low pay. Low pay measures of 50 per cent median and 75 per cent median produce very similar findings to our preferred definition of two-thirds median.

5   Figures for the years prior to 1994/5 are from Millar *et al.* (1997). These are not entirely consistent with the current study due to some differences in methodology, notably that the sample in the earlier study was limited to Great Britain and working-age adults.

6   Whilst the national minimum wage is currently set significantly below the low pay cut-off of two-thirds median hourly gross wages, if the level of the national minimum wage continues rising faster than median hourly wages, then in future the minimum wage and low pay measure will converge.

Chapter 3

1   DWP (2004) shows little change between 2001/2 and 2002/3.

2   Using the McClement's equivalence scale; see Appendix for further details.

3   This is the definition of a household in the 2000/1 FES; prior to that the definition was 'a single person or group of people living at the same address, which is their main residence, and who share meals or have common housekeeping'. This change in definition has resulted in an increase in the number of multi-adult households among groups of unrelated adults from 2000/1. This should not have a substantial impact on our results: Table 5 shows that, at most, 5 per cent of all employees and 5 per cent of low-paid employees in 2000/1 live in such households.

4   The figure of 11 per cent for 1994/5 is slightly lower than the equivalent estimate in our previous work (Millar *et al.*, 1997), where we presented a figure of 13 per cent. This difference is due to a revised methodology. For more details about the approach to measuring household poverty see the discussion of data and definitions in the Appendix.

5   See Appendix for more details of the benefits and tax credits which fall under the three headings.

6   Household-level deductions (such as council tax) and the adjustment to set negative household incomes to zero have been subtracted from the net market income of the individual in the household with the highest net market income (earnings, self-employment income and investment income). In the event of ties (six households) the deductions are made from the head of household's net market income. See Appendix for further details.

7   About 9 per cent of all employed lone mothers work under 16 hours per week (Barnes *et al.*, 2004), so these low-paid lone mothers are more likely than employed lone mothers in general to work short weekly hours.

Chapter 4

1   Albeit that these are based on a different rationale, which is related to the costs of living. See the websites at: http://www.telcocitizens.org.uk/; http://www.tuc.org.uk/; and http://www.church-poverty.org.uk/living_wage.htm

2   These are zero awards based on circumstances at time of claim and annual income reported by that point. These may be positive claims at other times of the year if their circumstances change, or by the time of the annual reconciliation.

3   The credit is made up of a basic element (per person) plus a couple/lone-parent element (per couple/lone parent). So, lone parents and couples with the same incomes and number of children receive the same amount in tax credits (other things being equal), although the family size is larger for couples (by one adult).

4   Hillman also argues that having the same credit for lone parents and couples may also create a disincentive for lone parents to re-partner (or create an incentive for someone to become a lone parent). However, there is little evidence that this is a real issue in practice, although Francesconi and van der Klaauw (2004) estimate that working families tax credit did lead to 'a significant reduction in single mothers' subsequent fertility and in the rate at which they married'. The latter effect was particularly strong among mothers of pre-school children.

References

Abrams, F. (2002) *Below the Breadline: Living on the Minimum Wage*. London: Profile Books

Balls, E., Grice, J. and O'Donnell, G. (2004) *Microeconomic Reform in Britain: Delivering Economic Opportunity for All*. Basingstoke: Palgrave Macmillan

Barnes, M., Willitts, M., Anderson, T., Chaplin, J., Collins, D., Groben, S., Morris, S., Noble, J., Phillips, M. and Sneade, I. (2004) *Families and Children in Britain: Findings from the 2002 Families and Children Study*, DWP Research Report 206. Leeds: Corporate Document Services

Bennett, F. and Hirsch, D. (2001) *The Employment Tax Credit and Issues for the Future of In-Work Support*. York: York Publishing Services for the Joseph Rowntree Foundation

Brewer, M., Duncan, A., Shepherd, A. and Suarez, M.J. (2003) *Did WFTC Work? Analyzing the Impact of In-Work Support on Labour Supply and Programme Participation*. London: IFS

Bryson, A. and Marsh, A. (1996) *Leaving Family Credit*, Department of Social Security Research Report No. 48. London: HMSO

Dickens, R. and Manning, A. (2003) 'Minimum wage, minimum impact', in R. Dickens, P. Gregg and J. Wadsworth (eds) *The Labour Market Under New Labour: The State of Working Britain*. Basingstoke: Palgrave Macmillan, pp. 210–13

DWP (Department for Work and Pensions) (2003) *Households Below Average Income: An Analysis of the Income Distribution from 1994/5 to 2001/02*. Leeds: Corporate Document Services

DWP (Department for Work and Pensions) (2003a) *Measuring Child Poverty*. London: Department for Work and Pensions

DWP (Department for Work and Pensions) (2004) *Households Below Average Income: An Analysis of the Income Distribution 2002/03*. Leeds: Corporate Document Services

Francesconi, M. and van der Klaauw, W. (2004) *The Consequences of 'In-Work' Benefit Reform in Britain: New Evidence from Panel Data*, Institute for Social and Economic Research Working Paper 2004-13. Colchester: University of Essex, http://www.iser.essex.ac.uk/pubs/workpaps/pdf/2004-13.pdf

Goode, J., Callender, C. and Lister, R. (1998) *Purse or Wallet? Gender Inequalities and Income Distribution within Families on Benefits*. London: Policy Studies Institute

Gregg, P. and Harkness, S. (2003) 'Welfare reform and the employment of lone parents', in R. Dickens, P. Gregg and J. Wadsworth (eds) *The Labour Market Under New Labour: The State of Working Britain*. Basingstoke: Palgrave Macmillan, pp. 98–117

Gregg, P. and Wadsworth, J. (2003) 'Workless households and the recovery', in R. Dickens, P. Gregg and J. Wadsworth (eds) *The Labour Market Under New Labour: The State of Working Britain*. Basingstoke: Palgrave Macmillan, pp. 32–9

Heasman, D. (2003) 'Patterns of low pay', *Labour Market Trends*, April, pp. 171–9

Hillman, N. (2004) 'Condemning a little less and understanding a little more', in *Overcoming Disadvantage: An Agenda for the Next 20 Years*. York: Joseph Rowntree Foundation

Hills, J. (2001) 'Does a focus on "social exclusion" change the policy response?', in J. Hills, J. Le Grand and D. Piachaud (eds) *Understanding Social Exclusion*. Oxford: Oxford University Press, pp. 226–43

HM Treasury (1998) *The Modernisation of Britain's Tax and Benefit System number 2, Work Incentives: A Report by Martin Taylor*. London: HM Treasury

HM Treasury (2000) *The Modernisation of Britain's Tax and Benefit System number 6, Tackling Poverty and Making Work Pay – Tax Credits for the 21st Century*. London: HM Treasury

HM Treasury (2004) *Budget Report 2004*. London: HM Treasury

IFS (Institute for Fiscal Studies) (2003) *Green Budget*. London: Institute for Fiscal Studies

Inland Revenue (2004) *Tax Credits Quarterly Statistics*. London: Inland Revenue

Jenkins, S. and Rigg, J. (2001) *The Dynamics of Poverty in Britain*, DWP Research Report No. 157. Leeds: Corporate Document Services

Jordan, B., James, S., Kay, H. and Redley, M. (1992) *Trapped in Poverty? Labour Market Decisions and Low Income Households*. London: Routledge

Kempson, E. (1996) *Life on a Low Income*. York: Joseph Rowntree Foundation

Kempson, E., Ford, J. and England, J. (1996) *Into Work? The Impact of Housing Costs and the Benefit System on People's Decision to Work*. York: York Publishing Services for the Joseph Rowntree Foundation

Low Pay Commission (2004) *The National Minimum Wage: Building on Success. Fourth Report of the Low Pay Commission*. London: The Stationery Office

Machin, S. (2003) 'Wage inequality since 1975', in R. Dickens, P. Gregg and J. Wadsworth (eds) *The Labour Market Under New Labour: The State of Working Britain*. Basingstoke: Palgrave Macmillan, pp. 191–200

McKay, S. (2002) *Low/Moderate Income Families: WFTC and Childcare in 2000*, DWP Report No. 16. Leeds: Corporate Document Services

McKay, S. (2004) *Lone Parents in London: Quantitative Analysis of Differences in Paid Work*, DWP In-house Report No. 136

McKnight, A. (2002) 'Low-paid work: drip feeding the poor', in J. Hills, J. Le Grand and D. Piachaud (eds) *Understanding Social Exclusion*. Oxford: Oxford University Press, pp. 97–117

McLaughlin, E., Millar, J. and Cooke, K. (1989) *Work and Welfare Benefits*. Aldershot: Avebury

Metcalf, D. (2002) 'The national minimum wage: coverage, impact and future', *Oxford Bulletin of Economics and Statistics*, Vol. 64, pp. 567–82

Millar, J. (2003) 'Gender, poverty and social exclusion', *Social Policy and Society*, Vol. 2, No. 3, pp. 181–8

Millar, J. (2004) 'Squaring the circle: means-testing and individualisation', *Social Policy and Society*, Vol. 3, No. 1, pp. 67–74

Millar, J., Webb, S. and Kemp, M. (1997) *Combining Work and Welfare*. York: York Publishing Services for the Joseph Rowntree Foundation

National Statistics (2002) *Living in Britain 2001*. www.statistics.gov.uk/lib2001, published 17 December

National Statistics (2003) *Low pay jobs: down 70,000 in year to spring 2003*, www.statistics.gov.uk/cci/nugget-asp?id=591, published 5 November

Office for National Statistics (2002) *Family Expenditure Survey 1994/5 to 2000/1*. Colchester, Essex: UK Data Archive (distributor), SN 3478

Rake, K. and Jayatilaka, G. (2002) *Home Truths: An Analysis of Financial Decision-Making within the Home*. London: Fawcett Society

Skinner, C., Stuttard, N., Beisel-Durrant, G. and Jenkins, J. (2002) 'The measurement of low pay in the UK Labour Force Survey', *Oxford Bulletin of Economics and Statistics*, Vol. 64, pp. 653–76

Stewart, M.B. (1999) 'Low pay in Britain', in P. Gregg and J. Wadsworth (eds) *The State of Working Britain*. Manchester: Manchester University Press, pp. 225–48

Sutherland, H. (2001) *The National Minimum Wage and In-Work Poverty*, DAE Working Papers No. 0111, Department of Applied Economics, University of Cambridge

Sutherland, H., Sefton, T. and Piachaud, D. (2003) *Poverty in Britain: The Impact of Government Policy since 1997*. York: Joseph Rowntree Foundation

Toynbee, P. (2003) *Hard Work: Life in Low-Pay Britain*. London: Bloomsbury

Vogler, C. and Pahl, J. (1993) 'Social and economic change and the organization of money within marriage', *Work, Employment and Society*, Vol. 7, No. 1, pp. 71–95

Webb, S., Kemp, M. and Millar, J. (1996) *The Changing Face of Low Pay in Britain*. Working Paper No. 25, Centre for the Analysis of Social Policy, University of Bath

Weir, G. (2003) 'Self-employment in the UK labour market', *Labour Market Trends*, Vol. 111, No. 9, pp. 441–51

Williams, F. (2004) *Rethinking Families*. London: Calouste Gulbekian Foundation

Work and Pensions Select Committee (2001) *First Special Report: Integrated Child Credit*, HC 292. London: The Stationery Office

Appendix: Data and definitions

Data

The data used for this study are from the Family Expenditure Survey (FES) for the (financial) years 1994/5 to 2000/1. The FES is a voluntary sample of a random survey of private households in the United Kingdom. The basic unit of the survey is the household and in 2000/1 6,637 households took part, representing approximately a 60 per cent response rate. Data are collected throughout the year to cover seasonal variations in income and expenditure. The FES collects information from individuals within households on income, expenditure and socio-economic characteristics.

Definition of the sample

We include observations for the whole of the UK. The sample is defined as people who are 16 and over whose primary economic status (self-defined) is a full-time or part-time employee who is at work or temporarily absent. A further restriction is that individuals only remain in the sample if they have a positive value for hourly pay (see below). The resulting sample is around 5,700 observations.

Definition of pay

Pay variables as described below have been defined for all the years of FES data we are using: 1994/5 to 2000/1.

Hourly pay

The Family Expenditure Survey, like most other data sets, does not include a direct measure of hourly pay. Hourly pay is calculated as normal gross weekly wage/salary from main job, including overtime and bonus earnings, divided by normal hours worked (including overtime) at main job.[1] Pay is adjusted to exclude any tax credits paid through the pay packet (this only applies after the tax credits were first introduced in 1999). We impose a further condition that the individual was paid last week/month, otherwise pay is set to zero. This is to ensure that we have a measure of pay which refers to the individual's current circumstances.

The choice of *normal* pay rather than *actual* pay is partly to try and capture how much people usually receive but is also determined by the way hours are measured in the Family Expenditure Survey, which is in respect of normal rather than actual hours and is available for main job only. This means that when we are looking at hourly pay we are confined to the main job only. When we look at weekly pay, however, we do include pay from any (up to two) subsidiary jobs, giving a more complete picture of weekly returns from work.

Since the introduction of the national minimum wage, there has been much discussion about the accuracy of hourly pay estimated from weekly pay and hours, rather than measured directly (Skinner *et al.*, 2002; Dickens and Manning, 2003). There seems to be a lot of measurement error in survey data – people tend to round up both their earnings and their hours and proxy respondents may not have very good knowledge of either. More recently, the Labour Force Survey has been used to collect direct hourly measures and these seem to be more accurate but are only available for about half of the sample.

For our purposes, measurement error is likely to be less of a concern, since such error disproportionately affects the data on the very lowest and highest hourly wages. Hence, while it may lead to overestimates of the numbers receiving very low levels of pay (such as the minimum wage), the impact of measurement error is lessened when we count the numbers of people with wages below a more generous low pay line (such as two-thirds median). This is because it is more likely to be the case that these wage earners would be below the line whether wages are measured accurately or with error.

Weekly earnings

We are precluded from looking at the influence of subsidiary jobs on average hourly pay by data limitations (the hours variables only refer to main job). In the case of weekly pay, however, it is clearly more important to include pay from subsidiary jobs. The maximum number of subsidiary jobs taken into account is two. For the main job, we used the same variable as for hourly pay (normal weekly gross wage/salary from main job). For subsidiary jobs, there is no equivalent 'normal' variable. Instead, there is only a current definition (amount last time paid) which is what we have used. Although we have a slight inconsistency between these definitions of pay for main and subsidiary jobs, this only affects a few observations – approximately 200 observations a year have non-zero amounts for pay from subsidiary jobs. Furthermore, the alternative would have been to adopt a different definition of pay for main job (to match the definition of pay for subsidiary jobs) and this would have created a more serious inconsistency between hourly pay and weekly pay.

Definition of household disposable income

Household income variables, as described below, have been created for the 1994/5 and 2000/1 FES.

The approach taken is to, as close as possible, replicate a Households Below Average Income (HBAI) definition of disposable household income before housing costs. The key features of this are:

- usual net earnings from employment

- profit or loss from self-employment income

- all social security benefits (including housing benefit)

- income from occupational and private pensions

- investment income

- maintenance payments if received directly

- income from educational grants and scholarships (including, for students, top-up loans and parental contributions)

- the cash value of certain kinds of income-in-kind (e.g. free school milk).

Income is net of the following items:

- income tax payments

- national insurance contributions

- domestic rates/council tax

- contributions to occupational pension schemes (including additional voluntary contributions) and any contributions to personal pensions

- all maintenance and child support payments

- parental contributions to students living away from home.

Negative incomes are set to zero.

However, it is important to note that we have not been able to replicate this definition precisely. Most notably, we do not have self-employment losses, only profits. Full details are given below.

Usual net earnings

The measure of net pay uses the same measure of gross pay as for weekly pay, so it is usual gross pay for main and subsidiary jobs if paid last week/month. For household income we do not apply the additional conditions that the individual is an 'employee' (see definition of sample).

To make pay net, we subtract any deductions from pay for income tax, national insurance contributions (NICs), occupational pension contributions, additional voluntary contributions, personal pension contributions, maintenance and separation allowance and educational fees or maintenance for a non-household member. We also add the cash value for luncheon vouchers and income from odd jobs.

Self-employment income

Self-employment income is defined as self-employment profit from main and subsidiary self-employment less income tax and NICs (class 2). We impose the condition that the individual has to be currently self-employed for self-employment income to be included (main job). Because of the way the FES variables are defined, self-employment losses cannot be included (to match the HBAI definition we should include them as negative income). Some individuals end up with negative self-employment incomes after the subtraction of tax and NICs.

Investment income

Investment income is defined to include interest from a National Savings investment account or National Savings ordinary account, interest from a bank or building society account, TESSA interest, ISA interest, interest/dividends from stocks/shares, interest from gilt-edged stock and war loans, public/private pension, annuity/trust/ covenant, rent from property and other unearned income. The last two components are unlikely to be net of tax (see separate deductions below).

Social security benefits

For our purposes we split benefits into three categories – tax credits, non-means-tested benefits and means-tested benefits. For benefits liable to income tax, these amounts are gross of tax.

Non-means-tested benefits

This includes child benefit, NI retirement pension, NI widow's pension, war disablement/widow's pension, contributions-based job seeker's allowance/unemployment benefit, Christmas bonus, statutory sick pay, statutory maternity pay, industrial injury disablement pension, incapacity benefit, disability living allowance (self-care and mobility components), maternity allowance, severe disability premium, sickness benefit, invalidity pension and guardian's allowance in 2000/1. In 1994/5 sickness benefit and invalidity pension were included and there was no incapacity benefit or guardian's allowance.

Tax credits

This includes working families tax credit and disabled person's tax credit paid direct or through the pay packet for 2000/1. In 1994/5, this includes the benefits which were replaced by tax credits: family credit and disability working allowance.

Means-tested benefits

These include housing benefit, council tax benefit (means-tested component, not the status discounts for single person, students etc.), invalid care allowance, income-based job seeker's allowance, income support, government training allowance, welfare milk, free school milk, maternity grant and any other benefit (includes back to work bonus etc.). In 1994/5, there was no income-based job seeker's allowance or council tax benefit.

Other income

Included in other income we have any regular allowance being received from outside the household if received at present, education grant, student top-up loan, children's income and benefits received from trade unions and friendly societies. Maintenance income is included in the 'regular allowance' variable.

Deductions

Deductions not already subtracted from income are split into two categories – those at the individual level (which we go on to subtract from individual market income) and those at the household level (which are deducted from the market income of the person in the household with the highest market income, unless otherwise stated).

Individual-level deductions are income tax paid direct and NI contributions paid by non-employees less any income tax refund. Obviously this only includes income tax and NICs that have not already been subtracted from earnings, self-employment income etc.

Household-level deductions include council tax (amounts payable after status discounts), domestic rates (Northern Ireland only), personal pension contributions and maintenance allowance expenditure. Data on council tax payments are available in 2000/1 but not for 1994/5 and even in 2000/1 they are average rather than actual amounts payable (calculated by pooling data from several local authorities within a region to preserve respondents' confidentiality).

Total income – treatment of negatives

In line with the HBAI methodology negative incomes are set to zero (affects 1 per cent of observations). Hence a new variable is created to capture this adjustment (since we want separate income components to add to the total and it is not obvious which income component should be adjusted). In the presentation of results for household income/poverty, this amount is deducted from the market income of the person in the household with the highest market income, unless otherwise stated.

Components of household income for our analysis

For the purposes of our analysis we create the following components of income:

- own market income: own earnings, self-employment income and investment income less individual deductions

- partner's[2] market income: partner's earnings, self-employment income and investment income less individual deductions

- household non-means-tested benefits

- household tax credits

- household means-tested benefits

- others' market income: earnings, self-employment income and investment income less individual deductions for person in the household other than self or partner

- household other income.

Household deductions and any adjustment for negative incomes are deducted from the market income of the person in the household with the highest market income, unless otherwise stated.

Equivalisation

Incomes are equivalised using the McClement's before housing costs equivalence scale.

Weighting

Grossing-up weights were applied to the data to adjust for differential non-response and generate representative population totals. The weights provided within the FES data were missing for 1994/5 and 1995/6 and hence we created our own grossing-up variables for each of the seven years of the FES data we use. This was done using population totals kindly provided by the Department for Work and Pensions. These population totals are for Great Britain and are broken down into eight categories on the basis of an individual's age, sex and marital status, jointly for England and Wales and separately for Scotland. Weighting factors were then calculated by dividing the population total for each category by the number of observations in that category in the FES data. Since population totals were not available for Northern Ireland (which is included in the FES sample) we applied the weights for England and Wales to Northern Ireland.

Sensitivity testing

Table A1 presents results for two alternative definitions of hourly low pay: 50 per cent median and 75 per cent median.

Table A1 Sensitivity testing of low pay measure

(a)   Hourly low pay 1994/5 to 2000/1 – 50 per cent median

	Hourly low pay threshold	% all low-paid	% men low-paid	% women low-paid	Relative risk women/men
1994/5	£2.88	8.2	5.4	11.3	2.1
1995/6	£2.97	7.8	5.6	10.2	1.8
1996/7	£3.09	9.0	6.3	11.9	1.9
1997/8	£3.23	8.9	6.7	11.3	1.7
1998/9	£3.29	9.2	6.8	12.0	1.8
1999/0	£3.51	8.2	5.8	10.8	1.9
2000/1	£3.65	9.2	7.2	11.5	1.6

(b)   Hourly low pay 1994/5 to 2000/1 – 75 per cent median

	Hourly low pay threshold	% all low-paid	% men low-paid	% women low-paid	Relative risk women/men
1994/5	£4.32	29.7	18.9	41.3	2.2
1995/6	£4.45	30.1	20.6	40.4	2.0
1996/7	£4.64	30.4	19.9	41.8	2.1
1997/8	£4.84	30.4	21.6	40.3	1.9
1998/9	£4.93	30.4	21.5	40.5	1.9
1999/0	£5.27	31.1	22.3	40.9	1.8
2000/1	£5.47	30.7	23.9	38.5	1.6

Verification of results on household structure

Differences in the definition of family unit and choice of sample make it difficult to directly compare our results on household structure and the proportion of employees living in a household with other families with those from other studies. However, on closer inspection our results for 2000/1 are consistent with those from the 2001 General Household Survey (National Statistics, 2002) and, for lone parents, with the findings presented in McKay (2004), using the 2001 and 2002 Labour Force Surveys (LFS).

Our definition of family unit is a single person or married or cohabiting couple plus, if there are any, dependent children. Dependent children are defined as those aged under 16, or aged 16 to 18 and in full-time education. Our sample is all employees aged 16 and over in the UK. Of these, we find that 34 per cent live in households where there are more than one family unit (Table 5). If, for the purposes of comparing our results with other studies, we widen our sample to all individuals in the UK, we find that 23 per cent of people live in households where there are more than one family unit (keeping other definitions the same).

In contrast, the definition of the family unit used in the General Household Survey (GHS) is a married or cohabiting couple or lone parent plus any dependent children and any non-dependent children as long as they are never married and childless (the definition of dependency is the same as that given above). Results for the GHS are presented for all persons in Great Britain, including children, and these show that 16 per cent of individuals live in what we would consider to be multiple-family households (two or more unrelated adults; couple or single person with non-dependent children only; two or more families). This is clearly significantly different from our result of 23 per cent of people living in households where there are more than one family unit.

However, in the GHS a further 45 per cent of individuals live in households which are comprised of couples or single parents plus dependent children and, if there are any, non-dependent children. According to our definition of family unit, non-dependent children are in a separate family from their parents, so an unknown proportion of this 45 per cent are also living in multiple-family households.

To be able to check more precisely whether our results from the FES are consistent with those from the GHS we generated additional results where the definitions are consistent with those presented in the text and Tables 5 and 14. This produced the following findings, which suggest that our results are comparable with those from the GHS:

- Ten per cent of people in the FES live in a household which is parent(s) plus non-dependent children only; this compares to 11 per cent in the GHS.

- Thirty-six per cent of people in the FES live in a household which comprises only a single person or a couple; this compares to 38 per cent in the GHS.

- Forty-nine per cent of people in the FES live in a household which is only parent(s) plus dependent children and, if there are any, non-dependent children; this compares to 45 per cent in the GHS.

- Ninety-four per cent of people in the FES live in a household which comprises only a single person or a couple plus, if there are any, dependent children and, if there are any, non-dependent children; this compares to 95 per cent in the GHS.

McKay (2004) shows that 9 per cent of lone mothers in the UK were living in households that contained more than one family unit in 2001/2 (based on analysis of combined 2001 and 2002 Labour Force Surveys).

In Table 5 we show that 28 per cent of lone-parent employees in the 2000/1 FES were living in a multiple-family household in the UK (of these very few were lone fathers). If we change our sample for the purposes of this comparison to all lone mothers, we find that 21 per cent of all lone mothers in the FES lived in households that contained more than one family. Again the discrepancy, in this case with the LFS, can be explained by the difference in definition of family unit. That used in the LFS includes non-dependent children in the same family as their parent(s) as long as the children are never married and childless; we always count non-dependent children as a separate family unit from their parent(s). When we exclude lone mothers living with dependent and non-dependent children only (13 per cent of lone mothers), we are left with 8 per cent of all lone mothers living in multiple-family households in 2000/1, which is very similar to the LFS result of 9 per cent.

Verification against Households Below Average Income

Table A2 gives a comparison of our results with those from the HBAI (which uses data from the Family Resources Survey). The following are the main differences between our methodology and that used for HBAI (other than those already noted above):

- HBAI excludes Northern Ireland and north of the Caledonian Canal in Scotland; our results are for the whole of the UK.

- HBAI excludes households where there is a temporarily absent spouse and where self-employed income accounts refer to a period over seven years ago.

- Using data from the Survey of Personal Incomes, adjustments are made to the number of high-income households and their income level; 'high income' is a gross income of £60,000 for pensioner households and a net income of £150,000 for non-pensioner households.

- The results excluding the self-employed are considered more reliable, hence we also produce results for 2000/1 which exclude individuals in households where someone is full-time self-employed. In 2000/1, this excludes 6.9 per cent of individuals in the HBAI analysis of the FRS and 10.8 per cent of individuals in our analysis of the FES.

- The HBAI uses grossing-up weights to adjust for differential non-response and produce representative population estimates. All the results in this study are weighted (for details see above) but the FES results in Table A2 are left unweighted because we have not created grossing-up weights for the entire population.

Table A2 Poverty rates in 1994/5 and 2000/1: HBAI and FES analysis compared

% individuals with incomes below

HBAI (FRS 2000/1)
Including the self-employed

Median			Mean		
50%	60%	70%	40%	50%	60%
10	17	26	9	19	30

Excluding the self-employed

Median (£290)			Mean (£350)		
50%	60%	70%	40%	50%	60%
9	16	25	8	17	28

This study (FES 2000/1)
Including the self-employed

Median (£282)			Mean (£333)		
50%	60%	70%	40%	50%	60%
13	20	28	12	19	29

Excluding the self-employed

Median (£280)			Mean (£324)		
50%	60%	70%	40%	50%	60%
13	20	28	11	18	27

% individuals with incomes below

HBAI (FRS 1994/5)
Including the self-employed

Median			Mean		
50%	60%	70%	40%	50%	60%
9	18	27	8	18	29

This study (FES 1994/5)
Including the self-employed

Median			Mean		
50%	60%	70%	40%	50%	60%
11	19	28	9	18	28

Notes

1 Observations are dropped if hours are zero but normal weekly pay for main job is non-zero. This affects four observations in 2000/1.

2 Partners are defined to be any other adult in the same benefit unit.